Freeing the Angel from the Stone:

A Guide to Piccirilli Sculpture in New York City

Jerry and Eleanor Koffler

The John D. Calandra Italian American Institute
New York

John D. Calandra Italian American Institute
New York

2008, Second printing

Library of Congress Control Number
2006924414

Cover Art: *Commerce and Industry* @ Rockefeller Center
Photo by Christine Roussel

ISBN
978-0-9703403-2-0
0-9703403-X

Contents

To the memory of Dr. Theodore L. Kazimiroff
Then there was light

and

To the memory of Phil Cannistraro
And gladly wolde he lerne, and gladly teche

ACKNOWLEDGMENTS

The authors wish to express their deep gratitude to numerous persons who have graciously assisted in this task.

List of Photographs

Page **Sculpture name and location**

29. *Carl Schurz Monument* @ Morningside Drive & 116th Street
Photo by Eleanor Koffler

30. Relief Panel: *Carl Schurz Monument* @Morningside Drive & 116th Street
Photo by Eleanor Koffler

31. Main Portal *Cathedral of St. John The Divine* @ Amsterdam Avenue & 112th Street
Photo by Jerry Koffler

32. Low Library /Columbia University
Photo by Jerry Koffler

34. Top photo: Main portal of Riverside Church @ Riverside Drive between 120th-122th Streets
Photo by Jerry Koffler
Bottom photo: Detail with Albert Einstein @ Riverside Church
Photo by Eleanor Koffler

35. Bruno Piccirilli working on models for Riverside Church
Photo courtesy of Riverside Church Archives

36. *Chancel Screen* in Riverside Church
Photo by Eleanor Koffler

37. *Firemen's Memorial* @ Riverside Drive & 100th Street
Photo by Jerry Koffler

38. Top photo: *Duty: Firemen's Memorial* @ Riverside Drive
Photo by Jerry Koffler
Middle photo: *Fortitude: Firemen's Memorial*
Photo by Eleanor Koffler
Bottom photo: Bas Relief: *Firemen's Memorial*
Photo by Jerry Koffler

40. *Maine Monument* @ Columbus Circle and Central Park West
Photo by Eleanor Koffler

41. Top photo: *Fortitude /Maine Monument*
Bottom photo: *Columbia Triumphant/Maine Monument*
Photos by Eleanor Koffler

43. Top photo: *Children of Prescott Hall Butler* @ Metropolitan Museum of Art
Courtesy of The Metropolitan Museum of Art, Gift of Jacob H. Schiff, 1905 (5.15.1) Photograph by Jerry Thompson. All rights reserved, The Metropolitan Museum of Art.
Bottom photo: *Children of Jacob H. Schiff* @ Metropolitan Museum of Art
Courtesy of The Metropolitan Museum of Art, Gift of Jacob H. Schiff, 1905 (5.15.3) Photograph by Jerry Thompson. All rights reserved, The Metropolitan Museum of Art.

44. Top photo: *Memory* @ Metropolitan Museum of Art
Courtesy of The Metropolitan Museum of Art, Gift of Henry Walters, 1919 (19.47) Photograph by Jerry Thompson. All rights reserved, The Metropolitan Museum of Art.
Bottom photo: *Angel of Death and the Sculptor* @Metropolitan Museum of Art
Courtesy of The Metropolitan Museum of Art, Rogers Fund, 1926 (26.113) Photograph by Jerry Thompson. All rights reserved, The Metropolitan Museum of Art.

45. Top photo: *Mourning Victory* @ Metropolitan Museum of Art
Courtesy of The Metropolitan Museum of Art, Gift of James C. Melvin, 1912 (15.75) Photograph by

Jerry Thompson. All rights reserved, The Metropolitan Museum of Art.
Bottom photo: *Fragelina* @ Metropolitan Museum of Art
Courtesy of The Metropolitan Museum of Art, Rogers Fund, 1926 (26.113) Photograph by Jerry Thompson. All rights reserved, The Metropolitan Museum of Art.

46. *Seal* at Metropolitan Museum of Art
Courtesy of The Metropolitan Museum of Art, Gift of Henry Walters, 1919 (19.47). Photograph by Jerry Thompson. All rights reserved, The Metropolitan Museum of Art.
Bottom photo: Frick Museum @ 70th Street & Fifth Avenue
Photo by Jerry Koffler. Copyright The Frick Collection, New York.

48. Top photo: *Orpheus* @ Frick Museum on 71st Street
Middle photo: Sculpture @ Frick Museum on 71st Street
Photos from Josef Lombardo's book *Attilio Piccirilli: Life of an American Sculptor*.
Courtesy of Dr. Jovin Lombardo.
Bottom photo: *Pulitzer Memorial Fountain* @ 58th Street and Fifth Avenue
Photo by Jerry Koffler

49. *Cornucopia: Pulitzer Fountain*
Photo by Jerry Koffler

50. Top photo: *Commerce and Industry* @ Rockefeller Center
Middle photo: *Youth Leading Industry*@ Rockefeller Center
Bottom photo: Joy of Life @ Rockefeller Center
Photos by Eleanor Koffler

Rockefeller Center photos courtesy of Tishman Speyer Properties

51. St. Bartholomew's Church
Photo by Jerry Koffler

52. *John Wycliffe/Capital* in St. Bartholomew's narthex
Photo by Eleanor Koffler

53. *Lion/* New York Public Library, Fifth Avenue & 42nd Street. Photo by Eleanor Koffler.
"The Potter Lions are a registered mark of The New York Public Library. Published with permission. All rights reserved."

54. Top photo: *Attic Figures/* New York Public Library 42nd Street & Fifth Avenue
Photos by Eleanor Koffler
Bottom photo:Morgan Library @ Madison Avenue & 36th Street
Photo by Jerry Koffler

55. Washington Square Arch @ Fifth Avenue in Washington Square Park.
Photo by Eleanor Koffler

56. Top photo: *Washington as Commander-in- Chief*
Bottom photo: *Washington as Statesman*
Photos by Eleanor Koffler

57. *Leonardo Da Vinci Art School* (St Nicholas Church @10th Street & Avenue A.)
Photo by Jerry Koffler

58. New York County Courthouse @ 60 Centre Street
Photo by Jerry Koffler

59. Top photo: Police Memorial Statue in NYC Police Headquarters
Photo courtesy of Dr. Jovin Lombardo

Bottom photo: New York Stock Exchange Pediment @ Broad Street.
Photo by Eleanor Koffler "used with permission of NYSE"

60. Detail of Pediment, New York Stock Exchange
Photo by Eleanor Koffler "used with permission of NYSE"

61. *Custom House* @ Bowling Green
Photo by Eleanor Koffler

62. *Belgium* @ Custom House
Photo by Jerry Koffler

63. Left top photo: *Asia* @ Custom House
Right top photo: *America* @ Custom House
Left bottom photo: *Europe* @ Custom House
Right bottom photo: *Africa* @ Custom House
Photos by Jerry and Eleanor Koffler

65. Brooklyn Museum @ Eastern Parkway
Photo by Eleanor Koffler

66. Top photo: *Brooklyn* @ Brooklyn Museum
Bottom photo: *Manhattan* @ Brooklyn Museum
Photos by Eleanor Koffler

67. Top photo: Detail of Pediment @ Brooklyn Museum
Bottom photo: *Kalidassa* @ Brooklyn Museum
Photos by Eleanor Koffler

68. *Manu* @ Brooklyn Museum
Photo by Eleanor Koffler.

69. Top photo: Brooklyn Eagle @ Brooklyn Public Library Eastern Parkway
Bottom photo: *Soldiers' and Sailors' Memorial Arch* @ Eastern Parkway
Photos by Jerry Koffler

71. *Civic Virtue* @ Union Turnpike & 82nd Avenue
Photo by Jerry Koffler.

73. The six Piccirilli brothers. Photo appeared in *The American Magazine* vol. no. 2 Feb, 1930, p.70.

Today the inhabitants of Willis Avenue may not be aware of the studios that once stirred universal fame, but perhaps some day a memorial tablet will mark the spot.

From: "Famous Piccirilli Studio Birthplace of Great Statues"
Bronx Press Review of July 22, 1982, by John McNamara

General Introduction

There is no shortage of guidebooks to New York City. So, "Why another one?" you might ask. And the answer is: this guidebook is an attempt to bring back to public awareness the extraordinary talents of the Piccirilli brothers, a family of sculptors, and their importance in the public art and architecture in New York City.

The Piccirilli brothers- Attilio, Ferruccio, Furio, Orazio, Getulio and Masaniello- were famous on many counts. But a problem arises in writing about them because, for the most part, they worked anonymously carving into marble a fully realized sculpture from clay models provided by architects and other sculptors. Carving anonymously for others has been a practice since the earliest days of sculpture making and so is the practice of having only the modeler's name attached to the carving. Anonymity is the hallmark of many Piccirilli carvings.

Some famous works that you may have seen in New York City that were carved by the Piccirilli brothers are: the lions in front of the New York Public Library on Fifth Avenue and 42nd Street; all the statuary on the Brooklyn Museum and *The Four Continents* in front of the Custom House at Bowling Green. Outside of New York City are dozens of sculptures carved by the Piccirilli brothers for other sculptors. Foremost among them is the statue of Abraham Lincoln in the *Lincoln Memorial* in Washington, D.C., along with the *Dupont Circle Fountain*. Sculpture for the State Capitols in Harrisburg, Pennsylvania and Madison, Wisconsin, as well as the façade of the California Building in Balboa Park in San Diego, California are all Piccirilli- carved

The Piccirilli brothers were well known to the architects and builders of their time for their achievements in the field of architectural sculpture and they were valued for their skill and reliability by the many architects and builders who contracted them to carve the sculptures planned for their buildings. Attilio Piccirilli, head of the family's carving studio, was the brother who became the most famous for his own work as a sculptor. Among his most notable achievements are the *Maine Monument* and *Firemens' Memorial* in New York City. He was also the subject of a biography by Josef Lombardo.[1] Furio Piccirilli was acclaimed for his sculpture and sculptural decorations of the Parliament House in Winnipeg, Canada and has a sculpture in black marble of a seal in the Metropolitan Museum of Art. Orazio Piccirilli created a number of sculptures. His *Black Eagle* was awarded the *Ellin P. Speyer Memorial Prize* by the National Academy in 1926. His brothers Attilio and Furio had been previous winners of this award. Getulio Piccirilli who at the age of eighteen carved the pedimental sculpture of the New York Stock Exchange for John Quincy Adams Ward also produced work of his own. Masaniello, sometimes Tom and other times Thomas Piccirilli, usually worked in collaboration with Orazio on architectural and sculptural decorations. Among their collaborative work are the classical and floral designs at the Custom House and the New York County Courthouse at 60 Centre Street, the California Building and the short lived Clark mansion in New York City. During the time he was in New York Ferruccio Piccirilli also worked on the Custom House decorations.

Along with bringing back the Piccirilli brothers to public awareness, another purpose of this book is to honor them publicly. Many people believe that some form of public recognition- a plaque, a renamed street, school, park, or other means of permanent honor should be given them.[2] Famous in their time, they seem to have been lost to the present.

A few comments, past and present, about the Piccirillis might give a better idea of what has been thought of them. In 1917 an art critic wrote:

> Comparatively unknown to the outside world, every sculptor values the exquisite workmanship of the 'Piccirilli Brothers,' from whose studio and workshop in the Bronx has issued many a masterpiece of marble carving. There are six brothers, all of whom learned the trade carried by them to such high perfection; while Attilio and Furio went further and became accomplished sculptors themselves. In the *Maine Monument*, therefore, as well as the *Firemen's Memorial* on Riverside Drive, one sees the creation of Attilio Piccirilli, carried out only by the brothers in their most accomplished style.[3]

A few years later another art critic commented:

> Interesting and important figures in the march of American sculpture at the present time are the six Piccirilli brothers, known from coast to coast in all large cities, wherever architects and sculptors congregate. Their work celebrates the natural bond between art and craftsmanship...the Piccirilli brothers who have brought us from their native land the whole art and craft and science and business of 'freeing the angel from the stone' [4]

Most recently a publication of the Metropolitan Museum of Art describes the Piccirilli brothers as being, "the foremost artist-carvers in New York at the turn of the century."[5]

Their gift to New York City, as you will soon see, is omnipresent and as permanent as the stone they carved.

This guide is only a selective sampling from the hundreds of monumental and architectural sculpture in New York City carved by the Piccirilli brothers. The rest, some difficult to find and see, will be in an appendix. The sculpture you will see on the tour will be both the Piccirillis' own work as well as work they carved for other sculptors. The Metropolitan Museum of Art on its information placards no longer ignores the fact that it was the expert hands of the Piccirilli brothers who carved four sculptures credited to Augustus Saint-Gaudens and Daniel Chester French in their collection. French and Saint-Gaudens were the outstanding sculptors of their time. The sculptures currently on display in the American

Wing are *Memory* (1917-19) and *The Angel of Death and the Sculptor* (1926) carved for French; and *The Children of Jacob H. Schiff* (1906-7) and *The Children of Prescott Hall Butler* (1906-7) carved for Saint-Gaudens. A fifth sculpture, on display in the American Wing carved by the Piccirilli brothers is *Mourning Victory from the Melvin Memorial* (1912-15). It was carved for Daniel Chester French and at the time of this writing credit for the carving is missing from the information placard.[6]

Other places and events enter into the Piccirilli story and excursions into architecture, history, and the like may make it seem that the text of this work is rambling. But we believe the digressions are useful to try to recapture a time, of not too long ago, that is forever past. So let us go then you and I with a short account of the Piccirilli family and the Piccirilli studio with some focus of attention on the Bronx.

2. The Piccirilli Family: Their Studio; The Bronx

Yet I will look upon thy face again
My own romantic Bronx, and it will be
A face more pleasant than the face of men
Thy waves are old companions, I shall see
A well-remembered form in each old tree
And hear a voice long loved in thy wild minstrelsy.[7]

The arrival of the English steamship *Roman,* out of London, in early June of 1888, at Boston harbor signaled the start of a new epoch in American sculpture. Arriving aboard the *Roman* were Giuseppe and Barbara Piccirilli with four of their seven children. The parents and their teenage sons Orazio, Getulio, Masaniello and a baby daughter, Iole had been preceded to this country by the older sons, Ferruccio, Attilio and Furio who had come to New York from London a few months earlier.

The Piccirilli family consisted of the parents Giuseppe Piccirilli, a talented marble carver and pointer, and Barbara Giorgi Piccirilli. Giuseppe, who was born in Rome, moved to his wife's village, Massa, in Tuscany, near the famous marble quarries of Carrara after their marriage. They had a daughter Iole (1885-1973) and six sons, Attilio (1866-1945), Ferruccio (1864-1945), Furio (1868-1949), Orazio (1872-1954), Masaniello (1878-1949), (also called Tom and variations thereof) and Getulio 1875-1945). The entire family was in the United States by 1888. All the sons were gifted sculptors. Attilio and Furio both studied at the *R. Accademia di Belle Arti* in Rome. Masaniello studied sculpture in Massa, Italy. Ferruccio, Getulio and Orazio were trained by their father. Orazio had further study with Eduard Roine in New York.

The arrival of the Piccirilli family in 1888 came at a fortuitous moment in the history of American sculpture and the arts in general as their coming coincided with a proliferation of public art and architecture in this country. Shortly after the Piccirillis arrived the World's Columbian Exhibition was held in Chicago in 1893 that gave renewed impetus to the City Beautiful movement. The emphasis of the City Beautiful movement, which encompassed the years 1890-1920, was not on city planning but on architecture with attendant sculptural decoration. Edwin Blashfield, a muralist of the time, best describes the ideals of the City Beautiful movement:

> The names of public buildings are the century-marks of the ages....wherever the footprints of the spirit of civilization have rested most firmly some milestones of human of progress have risen to be called the Parthenon or Notre Dame, Giotto's Tower or Louvre, and to teach from within and from without, by proportion and scale, by picture and statue, the history of the people who build it; to celebrate patriotism, inculcate morals, and to stand as the visible concrete symbol of high endeavor.[8]

Some of New York City's finest structures, erected between 1890-1920 that still stand, and still are, "visible concrete symbols of high endeavor," are the Custom House, (1907); Woolworth Building, (1913); Low Library at Columbia University, (1897); Appellate Division, New York State Supreme Court, (1900); New York Stock Exchange, (1903); Morgan Library, (1906); Main Branch of the New York Public Library, (1911); Maine Memorial, (1913); Audubon Terrace, (1908); Gould Memorial Library at Bronx Community College formerly New York University, (1909); Pulitzer Memorial Fountain, (1916); General William Tecumseh Sherman equestrian statue, (1903); Soldiers' and Sailors' Memorial Arch, (1892); and the Brooklyn Museum of Art, (1915). These are but a few of the many creations that came out of the City Beautiful movement. The Piccirilli brothers were involved in the creation of many of these New York City landmarks.

Attilio was the most famous of the brothers having achieved renown as a sculptor in his own right. Among his many public sculptures in New York City are the *Maine Monument* at Central Park West, the *Firemen's Memorial Monument* on Riverside Drive and *Youth Leading Industry* at Rockefeller Center. Getulio, the youngest of the brothers, ran the business for the family. At the age of eighteen he carved the pedimental group of the New York Stock Exchange. Furio won recognition for his black marble *Seal* now at the Metropolitan Museum of Art, as well as for many other works. Masaniello and Orazio were also active sculptors. Working together they were busily employed on the architectural and sculptural decorations for many prominent New York City buildings, including the Frick Museum, Riverside Church and St. Bartholomew's Church.

Ferruccio was an adventurer of sorts. He fought on the Greek side in their war with Turkey in 1897 and was in Italy throughout the First World War. When working with his brothers he did architectural and sculptural decorations. His son Bruno was the only Piccirilli offspring to work as a sculptor. Joseph, Ferruccio's other son was an architect at the firm of Carrere and Hastings.[9]

The Piccirilli family came to New York for reasons that are unclear, bankruptcy and opportunity are mentioned, and established their own sculpture studio in Manhattan. In 1890 Mrs. Piccirilli was taken ill and advised by her doctor to move to the more bucolic Bronx for its fresher air and greener surroundings.[10] The family moved to East 142nd Street near Brook Avenue where they bought some land and eventually established the largest sculpture studios in the United States. A small artists' colony nearby called Wilton may have figured in the Piccirilli's choice of this part of the Bronx. It is described in John McNamara's *History in Asphalt*, "as a small village east of present-day St. Mary's Park . . . comprised of small estates and picturesque homes, surrounded by shady dells and flower pots . . . . Writers, artists and musicians liked it for its countrified air and its proximity to New York City. It was locally called 'Actorville' as it attracted members of that profession."[11] The closeness to Manhattan, access to the railroad and water transport, as well as recent improvements in public transportation also may have been considered in the choice of the Bronx for their relocation.

In the1890s the Bronx was still mostly countryside with farms scattered throughout. Mott Haven, the section of the Bronx that the Piccirilli family moved to, covers almost all of the area south of East 149th Street between the East and Harlem Rivers. It was developed as a residential area for Manhattan jobholders and, by the time the Piccirillis arrived, had a major piano making industry. The Third Avenue El had been extended to East 132nd Street before the family arrived.[12] Increased access to public transportation may have contributed to a spurt of rapid growth in the Bronx. In 1904 the first subway reached the Bronx, whose population was then around ninety thousand. Irish, Germans, Jews and Italians were the main ethnic groups living in the area.[13] It was a time of a huge migration from Europe to America and a time of great change. Between 1880 and 1915 Italian immigrants came to this country in great numbers. By 1910 there were over 340,000 Italian-born residents living in New York City[14]. They were not greeted with open arms. Prejudice and discrimination was their lot.

There are some instances of anti-Italian bias directed at Attilio Piccirilli recorded in his biography by Josef Lombardo. In 1930 the governor of Virginia, John Garland Pollard, appointed two of his friends to look into getting a portrait bust of Thomas Jefferson for one of the niches reserved for famous Virginians in the rotunda of the state capitol at

Richmond and another life size statue of James Monroe for Ash Lawn the estate of James Monroe. At the suggestion of a museum curator both men went to the Piccirilli studio where a statue of Monroe was found and Attilio Piccirilli undertook the commission to make the bust of Jefferson. Attilio's sketches for the bust were rejected by the Art Commission of Virginia with hints that, "Attilio Piccirilli's work would never be welcomed and that it was not repudiated on purely aesthetic grounds."[15] The two appointees of the governor, angered by the Art Commission's actions, told the Commission that its approval was not necessary and placated Attilio who was unwilling to continue with the work.[16]

Attilio went back to working on the Jefferson bust feeling he needed to, "complete his model in the actual presence of the Houdon bust of Jefferson."[17] The Houdon bust of Jefferson was at the New York Historical Society. The Society denied permission offering an excuse that was a complete lie. The Society, then WASPish to the core, just didn't want anyone with a name like Piccirilli around. Threats by one of the gentlemen from Virginia to make the matter public changed the Society's mind.[18] Other difficulties with the Art Commission in Virginia led Attilio to angrily say, "The Governor is not the artist. I am the artist and I am not making a political statue. Your bigotry and ignorance are too much for any man. Tell the Governor to go to hell! Good-bye!"[19]
A strong inference of anti-Italian bias also can be made from the rejection by the Lincoln Memorial Commission of Daniel Chester French's suggestion to have the Piccirilli name put on the pedestal of the *Lincoln Memorial*.[20] Virulent anti-Italian and anti-immigration sentiments in this country were high around the time the Piccirillis settled in New York.

Giuseppe Piccirilli headed the Piccirilli marble-carving studio until his death in 1910 when Attilio assumed its direction. The studio, at 467 East 142nd Street, was the largest in this country and was host to thousands of visitors including

Presidents Theodore Roosevelt, Taft and Wilson. Working space at the studio was given to other sculptors. Augustus Saint-Gaudens and Daniel Chester French were the most famous American sculptors to have worked there. Daniel Chester French, who was primarily a modeler and not a carver, had sent his work to Italy to be carved until meeting the Piccirilli brothers shortly after they arrived. Michael Richman writes, "During the remainder of his career French would work compatibly with these carvers, and they would execute all but two of his marble commissions."[21] Going a step further beyond not carving one's own model is not modeling one's own clay model. John Quincy Adams Ward had Paul Wayland Bartlett make the models for the pediment sculpture of the New York Stock Exchange and a young Getulio Piccirilli translated the models into marble.[22] One of the many assistants of Augustus Saint-Gaudens wrote that, "Saint-Gaudens depended so little on skill of hand, valued so little the technical element in modeling that another hand was as good as his if it were responsive to his thoughts."[23]

It is normal practice for a sculptor to not carve his own sculpture. A model that the sculptor fashioned would be sent to a carver for the actual translation from model to full size sculpture. The process of enlargement is called 'pointing' and is of ancient origin. It is done with a device that allows for taking off the surplus material to within an eighth of an inch or less of the finished surface of the carving block. It is then abraded with different substances until the desired surface is achieved.[24] Josef Lombardo writes of the process

> Few sculptors voluntarily acknowledge their inability to carve, and rarely admit that their models are entrusted to others for completion. The practice of 'finishing' a marble carved by someone else is an attempt to camouflage a lack of ability or confidence. A statue properly "pointed" by a capable artist leaves little for the sculptor to finish. Rubbing the surface of a statue with pumice, scraping it here and there with a rasp, or treating

> the marble with acid, can hardly be called carving or "finishing".[25]

Early in the history of American sculpture many, if not most, American sculptors went to Italy to better develop their sculpting abilities and for the production and finishing of their work. Around 1835, the usual procedure in a sculptor's studio was for the sculptor to make the clay model. Modeling was considered the creative part of the process and it was the Italian assistants who usually finished the piece. While the name of the maker of the model can usually be found on the base of the statue, the carver who actually carved the marble into a finished statue is almost never identified.

One American sculptor working in Italy told his assistants to leave the last one-eighth-inch of marble surface so that he could remove it and "finish" the statue himself. He found the work so exhausting that he swore never to do it again. Beside, he admitted, the Italian craftsmen could do it better anyway. Sculptors, then, looked on casting in plaster and carving in marble as work unfit for the creative artist. Gentlemen did not get their hands dirty. Any question of artistic integrity at that time would have been looked on as absolute nonsense then.[26]

In 1860 Nathaniel Hawthorne in his novel, *The Marble Faun*, described much of the above-mentioned process of converting a clay model into a finished statue:

> Here [in the sculptor's studio] might be witnessed the process of actually chiseling the marble, with which (as it is not satisfactory to think) a sculptor in these days has very little to do. In Italy, there is a class of men whose merely mechanical skill is perhaps more exquisite than was possessed by the ancient artificers who wrought out the designs of Praxiteles himself. Whatever of illusive representation can be effected in marble, they are capable of achieving, if the object be before their eyes. The sculptor has but to present these men with a plaster cast of

> his design, and a sufficient block of marble, and tell them that the figure is embedded in the stone, and must be freed from its encumbering superfluities; and in due time, without the necessity of his touching the work with his own fingers, he will see before him the statue that is to make him reknowned. His creative power has wrought it with a word.
>
> In no other art, does genius find such effective instruments, and so happily relieve itself of the drudgery of actual performance; doing wonderfully nice things by the hands of other people, when it may be suspected they could not always be done by the sculptor's own. And how much of the admiration which our artists get for their buttons and buttonholes, their shoe ties, their neck cloths—and these at our present epoch of taste, make a large share of the reknown—would be abated, if we were generally aware that the sculptor can claim no credit for such pretty performances, as im-mortalized in marble! They are not his work, but that of some nameless machine in human shape. [27]

The Piccirillis, though of a later generation, almost certainly subscribed to the same belief about sculpting and carving. Writing about the Piccirillis and their arrival in New York, a former curator of American painting and sculpture at the Metropolitan Museum of Art wrote:

> It became unnecessary for American sculptors to go to Italy to have their sculpture translated into marble. It became unnecessary, in fact, for a sculptor to know anything about stone cutting, and some were quite content to model in clay and have all their stonework done by the Piccirillis. Some sculptors have been unduly reticent and touchy on this point, but as no one expects an architect actually to build every house he designs or a composer to play every instrument in the orchestra, there seems to be no good reason why this interesting mechanical phase of sculpture should not be better known.[28]

The arrival in New York in 1888, of the Piccirilli brothers put into place a first class sculpting system that America had mostly lacked, and the foremost American sculptors quickly availed themselves of the system.

It is not well known —though a part of Bronx history— that a number of important monuments in Washington, D.C. were made in the Bronx. About six blocks from where the Piccirillis lived and worked stood the ornamental ironworks of Jaynes, Kirtland & Company. The ironworks was located near Westchester and Brook Avenues and in steep decline in 1890 when the Piccirillis settled in the Bronx. In its heyday Jaynes, Kirtland made the Bow Bridge in Central Park and the dome atop the United States Capitol in Washington, D.C.[29]

The Piccirillis added another little known bit to Bronx history. In 1919, in their Bronx studio, the Piccirilli brothers completed the carving of the statue of Abraham Lincoln for the *Lincoln Memorial*, also in Washington. The one hundred and seventy-five-ton statue was made of twenty-eight interlocking pieces and assembled at the Washington site by the brothers.[30] After the Second World War the Piccirilli studio fell into decline just as had the Jaynes, Kirtland ironworks and for similar reasons. The times had passed them by and the new had little use for the old.

With some of this prefatory material now out of the way the tour of Piccirilli sculptural works in New York City can begin. The tour is a long one and could conceivably take a number of days to complete. It might be broken down into segments of your own making. In this guide the tour begins in the Bronx and moves sequentially from the Bronx mainland into Manhattan and then to the other boroughs. A car might be useful but the use of a New York Transit Authority MetroCard, good for all public transportation, is a better idea. The transit pass that is good for unlimited travel on the trains and buses of the transit system will go a long way in removing the hassle of driving and parking in this congested city. A transit pass for one day, for seven days or for a month is available at token booths or machines in any subway station. They are not sold on buses. It may be necessary to arm yourself with a good city map, as well as maps of the subway system and of the bus routes in each borough as this guide will take you to boroughs of the city that may be unfamiliar to you. The clerk in the subway can usually provide a subway map. Bus maps can be found on buses, in Transit Authority stores, one is in Grand Central Terminal, and sometimes in areas where tourist literature is displayed. Detailed travel directions will be given in these pages when necessary.

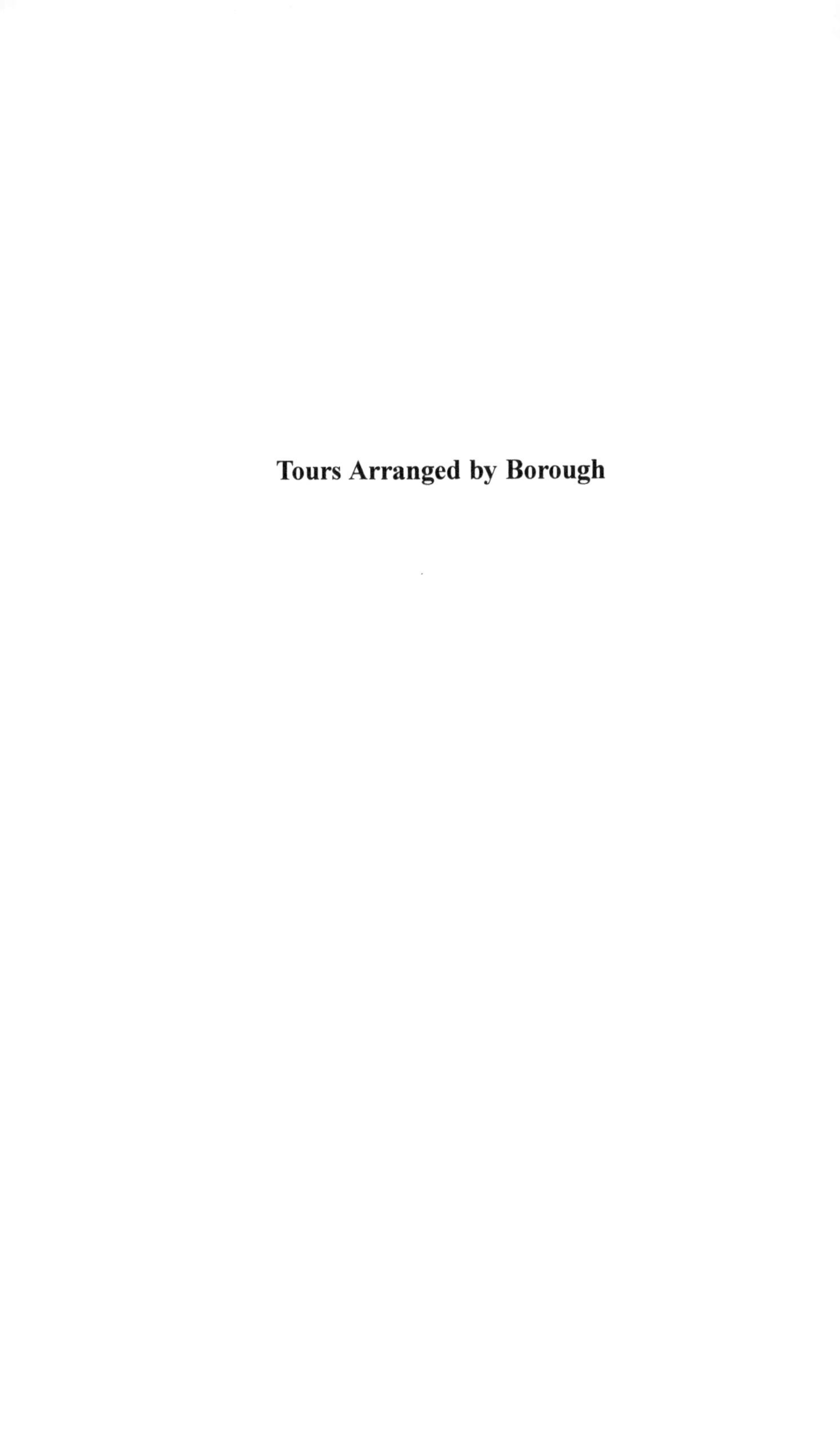

Tours Arranged by Borough

1. The Bronx

Why should the memories of the dead
Be ever those of gloom and sadness?
Why should their dwelling not be made
'Mid scenes of light, and life, and gladness?
Here let the young and the gay repair.
And in this scene of light and beauty,
Gather from Earth and Sky and Air,
Lessons of Life, and Love and Duty![31]

Woodlawn Cemetery in the Bronx, which dates from 1863, is a part of the nineteenth century's response to the overcrowded eyesores that city burial grounds had become and to the city's population's fears that cemeteries gave off poisonous and noxious gases. The solution was to bury the dead a distance from the city in what were termed "rural" or "garden cemeteries." Cemeteries became well-tended, beautiful parks of trees, and shrubs, and flowers where the dead were buried in a sort of well maintained, and even policed, botanical garden and arboretum.[32] In a 1960 survey of its trees Woodlawn listed 3,388 trees, not including ornamentals. Birdwatchers, several years ago, reported 119 species.[33] Pick up a copy of the map of Woodlawn Cemetery and the insert. The map has directions to notable gravesites and the insert whose cover reads; "The Woodlawn Cemetery" and whose actual title is; "Woodlawn: An Oasis of Art, History, Beautiful Ecology and a 'Hall of Fame.'" has directions to notable gravesites. The map with insert and other information are available at the Woodlawn Cemetery Office near the Webster Avenue entrance. Woodlawn is the permanent home of the rich and famous and of the extraordinary mausoleums that they built for themselves. Don't miss seeing some of them and the many notable graves. Among the mausoleums F.W.

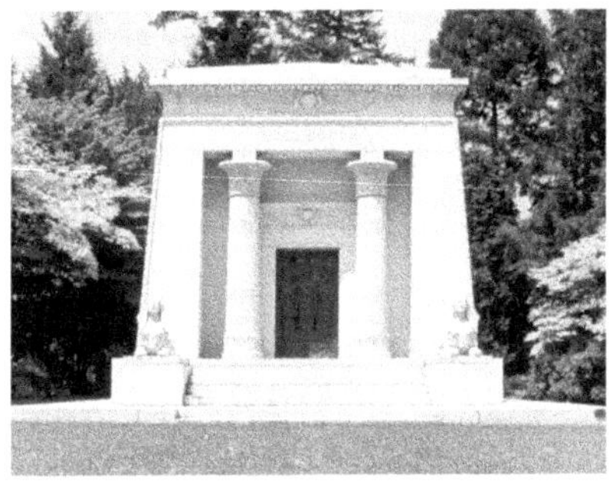

Woolworth's, a bit of ancient Egypt in New York, is a fine example of moneyed ostentation. Starting in 1879 Woolworth founded a chain of over 2,000 five-and-ten cent stores that only recently went out of business. His "Cathedral of Commerce," the Woolworth Building at 233 Broadway, near City Hall, is also well worth visiting inside and outside. Not to be outdone in ostentation and flamboyance Jules Bache, a financier, resides in a copy of the temple of Isis at Phylae, Egypt. Besides ancient Egypt there are dozens of examples of the glory that was Greece and the grandeur that was Rome among the numerous mausoleums. And there are many more magnificent mausoleums to see. You want Leonardo Da Vinci in the Bronx? The mausoleum of Oliver Hazard Perry Belmont is an exact replica of the Chapel of St. Hubert in France that Leonardo Da Vinci designed for his own burial. Belmont was both financier and horse lover, as was his father, August Belmont, before him. August Belmont founded the Belmont Stakes, which were first held in Jerome Park in the Bronx in 1867. Belmont Park racetrack is named for the family. Alva Smith Belmont (1853-1933) the wife of Oliver Hazard Perry Belmont is in the mausoleum with him. Alva Belmont devoted herself to

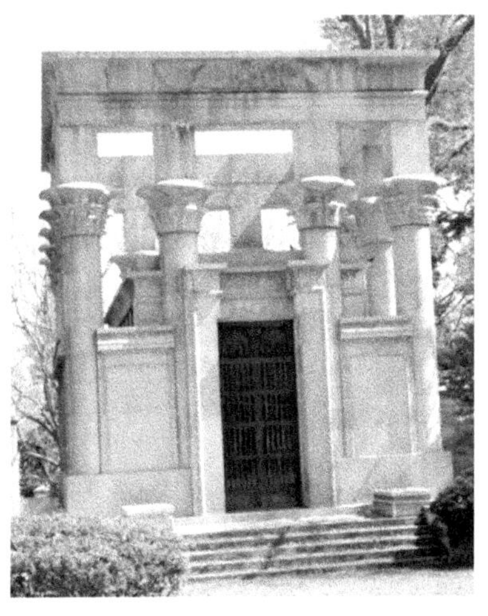

women's suffrage. Her motto was "Failure is impossible." She was President of the National Woman's Party from 1921 until her death in 1933. Its headquarters building, donated by Alva, is just behind the Supreme Court in Washington. Women were in charge of Alva's funeral, and in the mausoleum is her suffragette banner.[34]

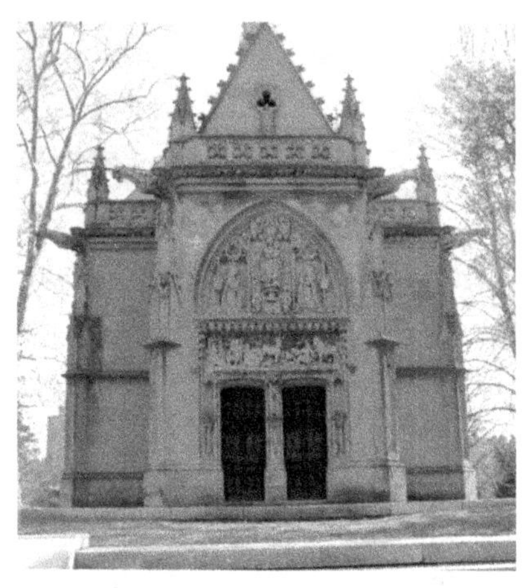

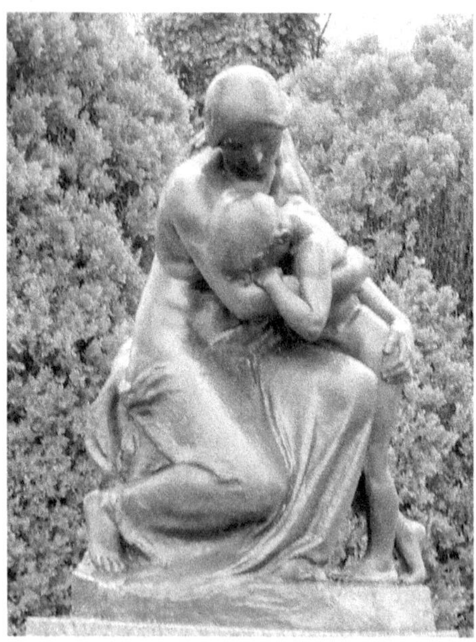

In Woodlawn Cemetery near the juncture of North Border Avenue and Elder Avenue (see the aforementioned map, available at the Woodlawn Cemetery Office) is a bronze sculpture, a copy of part of *The Maine Monument*.[35] The sculpture is by Attilio Piccirilli and shows a grieving mother and child. It originally marked the grave of Barbara nee Giorgi Piccirilli mother of the Piccirilli family of six brothers and a daughter, and the grave of her husband Giuseppe. Today the sculpture, an uninscribed marker, is the only indication that this is the site of sixteen burials of at least three generations of the Piccirilli family. Some mystery surrounds this gravesite marked only by the sculpture of the grieving mother and child. Why is it that there is not one word or any other indication given, beside the sculpture, to show that sixteen persons; Piccirillis, Miletis, Bernsteins and an Esposito, are interred there? Did they all enter into a silent compact for eternal anonymity for some reason?

In an interview with Albert Piccirilli, son of Masaniello one of the Piccirilli brothers, appearing in the *The Daily News* of November 2, 1985, the interviewer, Dan O'Grady wrote, "For reasons of their own, the Piccirilli brothers refused to pass on their artistic tradition to their children," Albert Piccirilli adds, "When the Piccirilli brothers died off, they wanted that to be the end of the Piccirilli's statues and marble works."[36] Perhaps so. But there are other unanswered questions or mysteries about this once famous family of sculptors. What happened to their business records? No one seems to know. Of the multitude of sculptures and decorations that beautify so many buildings in the city which did the Piccirilli brothers do? Why the rapid descent from famed to forgotten? Could it be that the brothers had a remarkable prescience about the future course of their style of sculpting and that the human figure was about to vanish?

There are four more sculptures by Attilio Piccirilli to be seen in Woodlawn Cemetery and there are at least three more that the Piccirilli Brothers Marble Carving Studio carved for other artists.

First is Attilio's own work a marble copy of the *Mother and Child* that we just saw at the Piccirilli grave. This mother and child marks the DeBlasio Memorial. To find this monument turn into Lake Avenue off Central Avenue going eastward until Lake Avenue becomes Ravine Avenue. Keep going until you reach the Clarence Day Monument which is at the corner of Observatory and Ravine Avenues. Continue

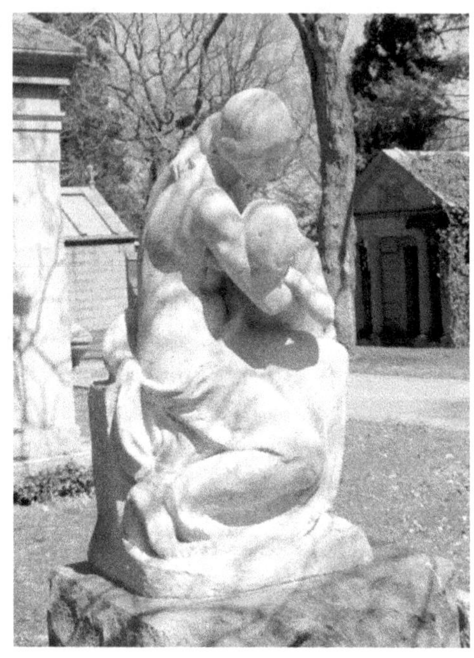

about 100 feet more on Ravine Avenue and you will find the DeBlasio Memorial. A similar statue of a mother and child was used by Attilio Piccirilli on the *Maine Monument* and the *Firemen's Memorial.* The DeBlasio statue might have been in the Piccirilli Studio when it closed and was placed on the DeBlasio grave in 1947.

The next sculpture and Atillio's most powerful work *The Outcast* is next. You will have to do a bit of searching for this grave as it is amidst many others in a plot named Myosotis at Prospect and Walnut Avenues, which are off Central Avenue. At the Myosotis Plot are the mausoleums of Paul Smith Jr. and Holzmaister. Behind and above these mausoleums is the Bulova Mausoleum. The grave you are looking for is behind Bulova. It is the grave of Ensign Nathan Piccirilli (1918-1944). Nathan Piccirilli was the son of Orazio and his wife Angelina both of whom are also buried at this site. Nathan was killed in World War II at the Battle of Ormac Bay in the Philippine Islands. The sculpture that marks his grave is by his uncle, Attilio Piccirilli, who died less than a year after his nephew at the age of seventy-nine. *The Outcast* is a powerfully evocative sculpture of a young man clutching himself in intense grief. It goes by many names: *The Outcast, The Pariah* and *The Friendless Immigrant*. The original, which this may be, was exhibited in many places here and abroad. It won the Gold Medal

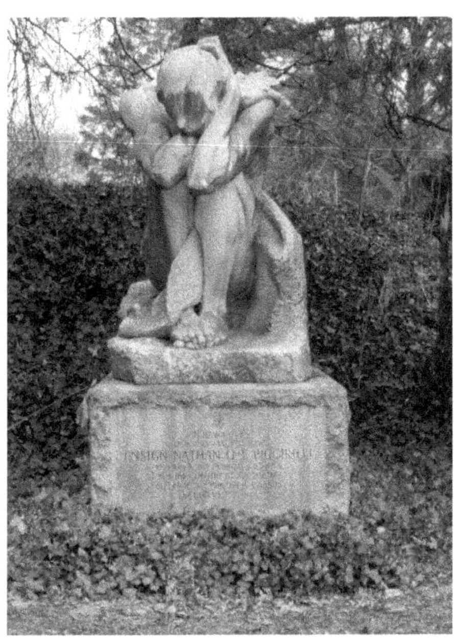

at the Panama-Pacific International Exposition in San Francisco in 1915.[37]

Although there were a number of copies of this sculpture the one in Woodlawn is the only known survivor. The Woodlawn version also presents something of a mystery. Nathan Piccirilli died December 7, 1944 and Attilio Piccirilli died October 8, 1945 and both were buried soon after death. But *The Outcast* was not put into place until 1947.[38]

The third work, simpler in conception, is less affecting as sculpture but we find its story still saddens many who hear it. Not too far away from the Nathan Piccirilli grave is the burial place of the first wife and infant daughter of Fiorello H. LaGuardia. There are many who consider LaGuardia New York City's greatest mayor. LaGuardia was elected mayor in 1933 but his character had been already formed by his experiences in Arizona as a child and his early jobs in Trieste, Budapest and Ellis Island as well as his military service in World War I. Along the way he learned to speak six languages and his liberal philosophy and reformist tendencies took shape.[39] Progressive in his political beliefs, scrupulously honest and a champion of the poor and of minorities, LaGuardia is still remembered as the agent of great change that brought about New York City as we know it A large bronze commemorative plaque sculpted by Attilio Piccirilli, who was a close friend of LaGuardia, marks the grave. Attilio had known both Fiorello and his wife well.

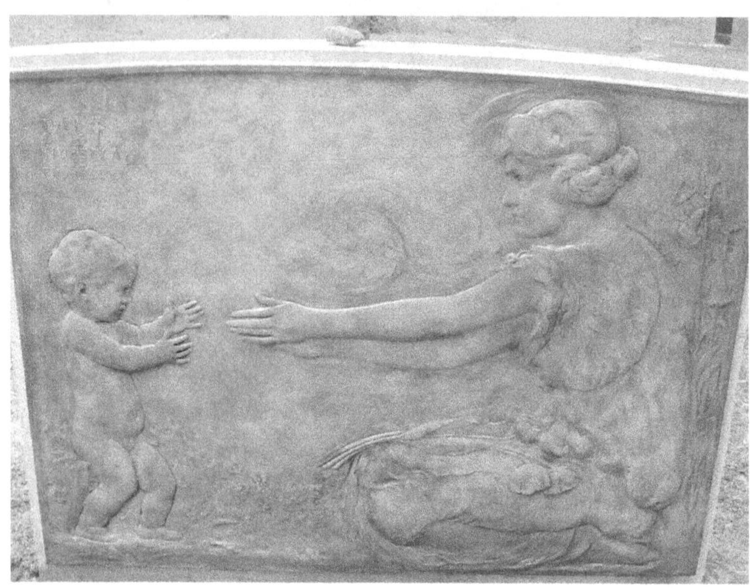

Attilio Piccirilli was one of a circle of close friends of the Little Flower (from his first name, Fiorello) and an early political supporter. In 1914 when LaGuardia was picked to run for Congress by the Republican Party he opened his election headquarters in a building owned by the Piccirilli family. Attilio Piccirilli campaigned for him and despite the violence of electoral politics at this time Attilio, "holding aloft a banner with LaGuardia's name, led a parade of some twenty persons during a pouring rain on Fourth Street, where they were picked off by Tammany braves with vegetables, rotten eggs, and other campaign grapeshot."[40]

The grave of Thea LaGuardia and her daughter Fioretta Thea is at I-1 Lotos, on the map. Though Fiorello's name is also on the grave marker, he is buried elsewhere in Woodlawn.[41] The grave of Mrs. LaGuardia is on Fern Avenue just before it merges with West Border Avenue. Look for it behind the Pohle Mausoleum. Within the plot is the Piccirilli grave marker, a bronze bas-relief showing a young mother reaching out to her child. The bas-relief is described in Lombardo's book:

> The mother is shown seated in a field of flowers with outstretched arms, beckoning her child to walk towards her. With faltering steps, the child moves hesitantly forward in an attempt to reach its mother. Several long-stem roses symbolizing love rest across the mother's lap. Tall, full-grown lilies, representing peace in death, rise mournfully behind her. The child is pictured in a patch of budding flowers from which it seems to emerge. Aside from its too pictorial character, the design of the bas-relief is very decorative and expresses a gentle sentiment.[42]

Thea Almerigotti married LaGuardia in 1919, around the start of his political career, when he was thirty-six and she was twenty-four. On the same day and in the same church Enrico Caruso also got married. Caruso was a close friend of both LaGuardia and Attilio and frequent guests at one another's homes. Were the marriages on the same day planned or coincidence?

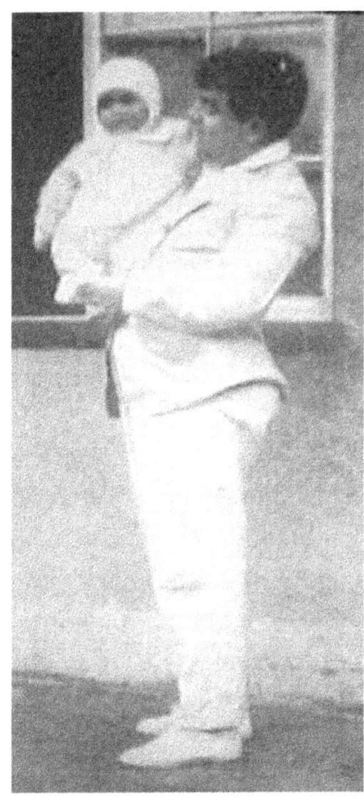

LaGuardia was described, in his marriage, as "ecstatically happy" and he, "who was enormously fond of children, lavished on his own child the love of a man who comes late to fatherhood."[43] But his joy was not to last. In 1921 both Thea and the infant died of tuberculosis, six months apart. His grief was inconsolable. To help him forget his sorrow and despair his friends arranged a trip to Havana, Cuba. Attilio Piccirilli accompanied him. In his grief LaGuardia conceived of the deaths of his wife and child as "victims of social murder" and when a reporter asked him if he knew how to improve New York City he excitedly replied:

> Could I! COULD I! he boomed. Say! First I would tear out about five square miles of filthy tenements, so that fewer would be infected with tuberculosis
> like that beautiful girl of mine—my wife, who died—and my baby—I would establish
> 'lungs' in crowded neighborhoods—a breathing park here, another there, based on the density of the population.
>
> Milk stations next! One wherever needed, where pure cheap milk could be bought for babies and mothers learn how to take care of them...[44]

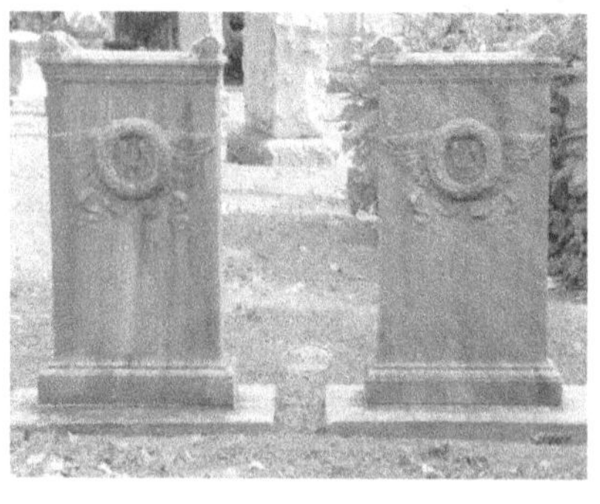

While looking through records at Woodlawn Cemetery, Susan Olsen, Director of The Friends of Woodlawn found the foundation order for the graves of Edwin Blashfield, an important muralist and art critic and his wife Evangeline. Attilio Piccirilli designed the grave markers and they were carved by the Piccirilli Brothers Marble Carving Studio. The Blashfield graves can be found in Woodlawn Cemetery in the Aster plot. Not far from Border Avenue on Park Avenue is the path leading to the Blashfield graves. Walk along the path which starts with the Boldt obelisk on the left and the Thomas Dimond mausoleum on the right. Continue along the path for a few more feet and the *Blashfield Memorial* is on the right, just after the George H. Shaffer mausoleum.

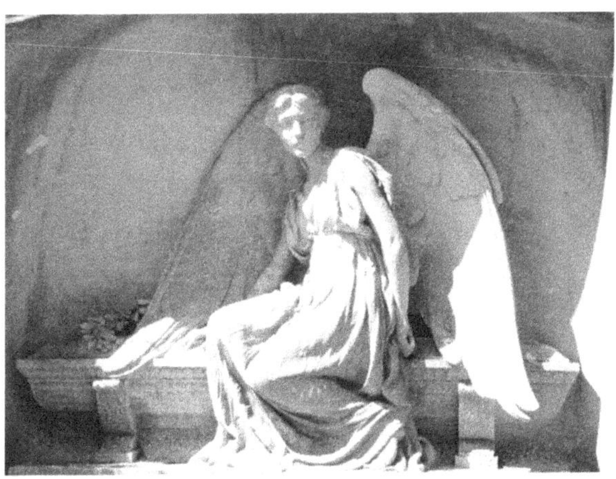

In Woodlawn Cemetery, the three other works that were carved by the Piccirilli Brothers Marble Carving Studio are the Kinsley, Bliss and Stransky Memorials. *The Kinsley Memorial* by Daniel Chester French has a figure of a beautiful angel seated on a sarcophagus and can be found off Central Avenue near Prospect Avenue in the Hawthorne Plot. The Kinsley Memorial is directly across the road from the large Foster Memorial. There is a large beech tree and the J.Edward Simmons Monument to the right. *The Kinsley Memorial* by Daniel Chester French, an outstanding work, was commissioned by the Kinsley family in 1911. The Piccirilli Brothers Marble Carving Studio carved this monument from Pink Tennesse Marble and has the D.C. French name on the monument. The Piccirillis carved most of D.C. French's work and they were greatly admired and respected by him. Placed next to the angel on the *Kinsley Memorial* are an hourglass symbolic of life's end and the laurel symbol of immortality.

The next place to be visited will be the *Bliss Memorial* by Robert Aitken which has tall standing figures of a man and a woman on a curving exedra. The memorial was carved by the Piccirilli brothers. It is located on a hillside, opposite the Straus

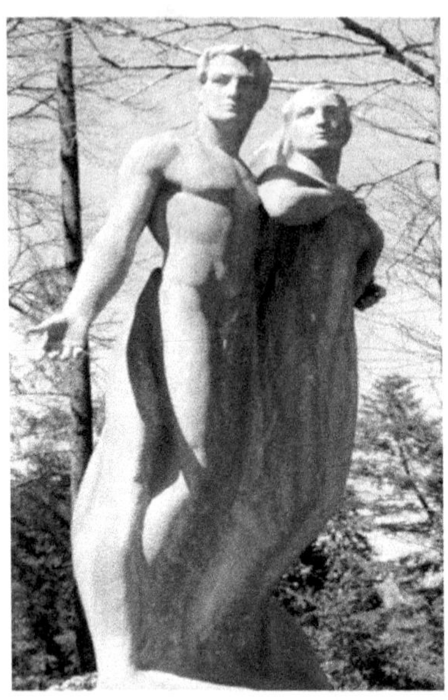

Memorial in the Walnut Plot off Myosotis Avenue.

The *Straus Memorial* is a memorial to Ida and Isidor Straus who were lost when the Titanic sank and the *Bliss Memorial* may have also been a tribute to people lost on the Titanic. Anna Bliss commissioned Robert Wells Bosworth, architect for the Rockefeller's Kykuit Estate, to design the wave-like exedra. Robert Aitken, won the competition for the sculpture to be placed on the pedestal. The *Bliss Memorial* was designated Monument of the Year in 1918.

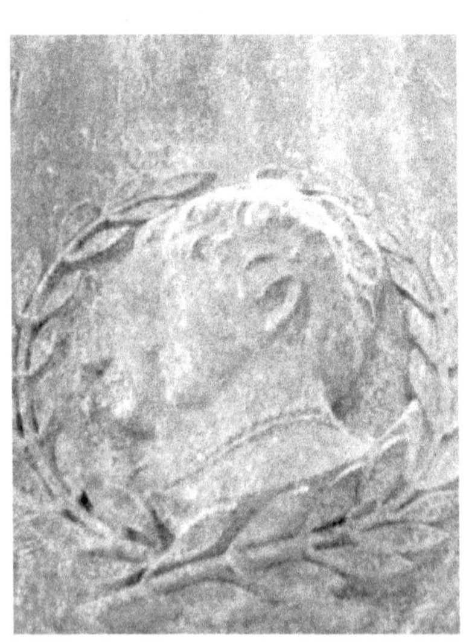

The Stransky Monument, the last work we will look at in Woodlawn Cemetery was designed by Mario J. Korbel and carved by the Piccirilli brothers. It is in the Arbutus Plot off Myosotis Avenue near Park Avenue. It is difficult to see for it is hidden behind a giant ginko tree and several bushes. Directly across the road is the *Havender Mausoleum*. Other monuments which help you locate the *Strankský Monument* are: to the left the *Perrella Mausoleum* and to the right the *Gainsburg Mausoleum.* The *Stransky Monument* is a marble monument that has deteriorated. On the front of the monument are carved the profile heads of Josef and Marie Stransky. A musical score is carved into the stone, perhaps a requiem by Stransky who was a conductor of the New York Philharmonic Orchestra from 1911 to 1923.

We leave Woodlawn for the Belmont section of the Bronx centered around East 187th Street and Arthur Avenue. Although the neighborhood is still predominantly Italian there has been a heavy influx recently of Albanians and others from what formerly was Yugoslavia, as well as, of Blacks and Hispanics to the area. A mosque, of recent construction, opened not too long ago. The area's strength has been its ability to resist the plagues that have infected most of the city, crime and drugs. The Belmont area is most busy on weekends when people come from all over do their food shopping in the many attractive stores. Tourism to the area has also picked up considerably in recent times. Community pride is still strong, as it has been from its earliest times.

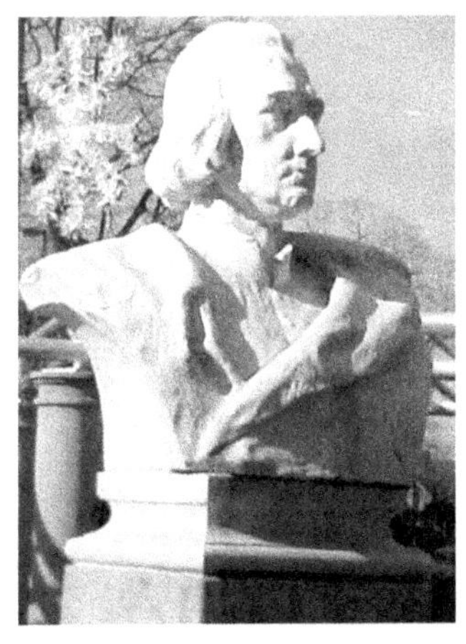

In the heart of the Belmont area, at the intersection of Crescent and Arthur Avenues is D'Auria-Murphy Park. This park contains a bust of Christopher Columbus sculpted by Attilio Piccirilli. The sculpture was dedicated on October 13, 1925 in an unveiling ceremony that was described as being, "like an Old World religious festival."[45]

According to LaGuardia's biographer "A parade of three thousand members of various Italo-American societies snaked its way through the Latin quarter to Columbus Square, where LaGuardia, speaking in both English and Italian to an audience of fifteen thousand, celebrated Italian explorations, Italian art,

Italian genius, and Italo-American contributions to the United States."[46]

The sculpture has been moved a number of times since its dedication. Its original location, a small park, now gone, was at 189th Street and Lorillard Place opposite P.S. 45. The principal of the school was Angelo Patri a noted educator and the first Italian-American principal in this city. Patri was another of a number of close friends of Attilio Piccirilli and a prominent member of the Italian-American community.

After viewing the sculpture, we shall now snake our way through this Latin Quarter, one of the better Little Italies in New York City. Check the food stores along Arthur Avenue and if you are hungry try a slice of pizza; or have a complete Italian meal in one of the many restaurants. There are many interesting stores both for food and other specialties. Visit the church, Our Lady of Mount Carmel, which in the 40's and 50's had more than 40,000 members; and, though difficult to find open, the mosque on the corner of Belmont Avenue and East 189th Street. The recent influx of Albanians to the neighborhood has introduced some of their food specialties to the area. Try a slice of *borek* at Tina and Tony's Pizzeria, 2479 Arthur Avenue at East 189th Street. *Borek* is a phyllo type dough variation of pizza that is filled with a choice of meat, cheese or spinach. We favor the spinach. For a slice or two of very good pizza try the Full Moon Pizzeria at 600 East 187th Street. Since we live within walking distance of the Belmont neighborhood and shop for much of our fresh food in this area here are a few other recommendations. Biancardi for meat, 2350 Arthur Avenue; heavenly, fresh bread at Addeo, 2372 Hughes Avenue, or at their second store next door to Biancardi; Casa Della Mozzarella, an Italian deli, 604 East 187th Street can provide hero sandwiches, sandwich meats, cheeses and other divine Italian specialties. For freshly made ravioli and egg noodles go to Borgatti's, 632 East 187th Street. Nourished and restored we leave for the island of Manhattan.

2. Manhattan

> There, gaping before us were the jaws of the iron dragon: the immense New York metropolis.[47]

Our tribulations in the Iron Tower of Babel have begun.[48] By our reckoning there are over 500 (See Appendix 2) works in Manhattan that are attributable to the Piccirillis. We will visit but a handful and begin at the *Carl Schurz Monument* on Morningside Drive and West 116th Street. The bronze sculpture was done by Karl Bitter and unveiled in 1913. Henry Bacon was the architect. The Piccirilli brothers did the granite reliefs that were designed in Greek archaic style by Bitter. The reliefs are below the statue and on either side of it.

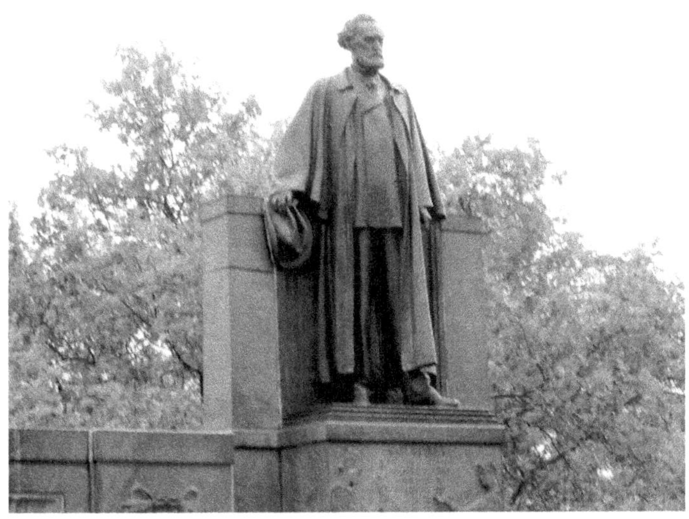

In his relatively short life, Karl Bitter, an Austrian, was successful in most of his undertakings. Possibly, his determination to prove his father wrong provided the impetus for his achievements. Bitter's father wanted his sons to become lawyers and when the young Bitter took himself out of regular school to enter art school in Vienna his father almost disowned him. Bitter had hoped to become a landscape painter but was misdirected to a modeling class and found his true calling. He came to America in 1889 after deserting the army and found almost instant success as a modeler, carver and sculptor.[49]

Carl Schurz (1829-1906), the subject of the monument, was born in Germany and came to the United States in 1852. Schurz had a varied career that included serving as a senator from Missouri and fighting in the Civil War as a Major General. He was at different times a newspaper correspondent and as editor and owner of a newspaper he was almost always involved in politics. Schurz was: a spellbinding speaker, a political reformer, opposed to slavery for fairness to American Indians, and, as the inscription on the central relief panel says, "A Defender of Liberty and a Friend of Human Rights." The relief panels illustrate these themes.

The relief panels are of gray granite and were carved by the Piccirilli brothers. The central panel shows a male and

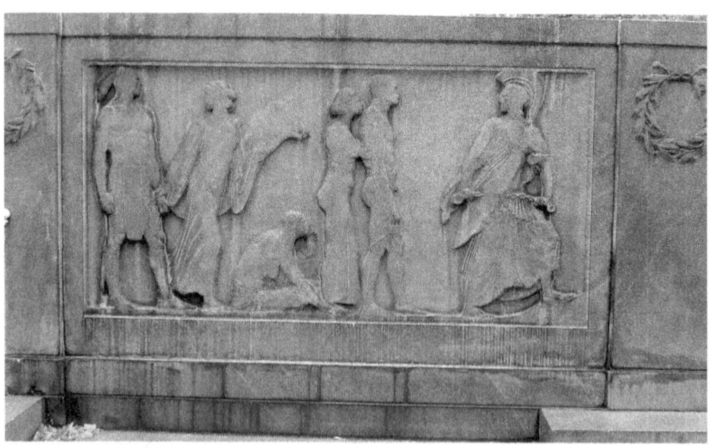

female figure. He is the defender of liberty, with sword, while she represents the friend of liberty, through gesture. In the left panel a Greek warrior (Bitter came late to his interest in Greek archaic style) breaks the chains of slavery and you go figure out what the female figure has in mind for the Indians. The interpretations vary. In the right panel Liberty is shown leading the people, a reference to Schurz' interest in civil liberties. In a paean to the combined talents of Bitter and Piccirilli appearing in a 1917 book the panels were described as, "those astonishing reliefs so eloquently cut into the hard, black granite at the ends of the exedra. There is nothing like them in American art."[50]

According to some close associates of Karl Bitter this might not be the same statue of Schurz that was unveiled in 1913. The original had shrunk more than expected during the casting process and, at his own expense, a dissatisfied Bitter (maybe a bitter Bitter, *bitte*) made a better proportioned casting and in the middle of the night made the swap.[51]

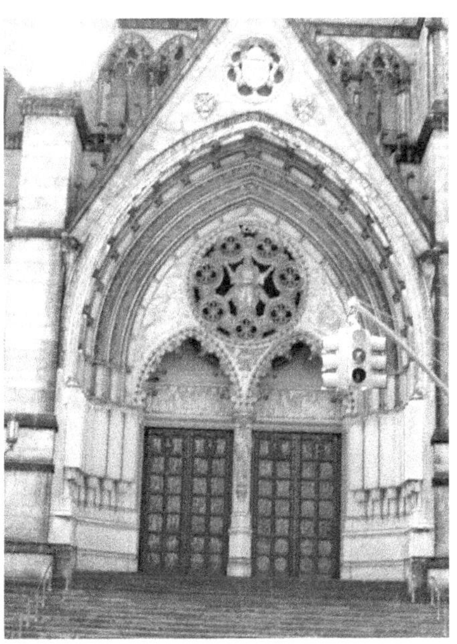

Our next stop is the Cathedral Church of Saint John the Divine. Construction on the Cathedral began in 1892 and it is still far from finished. The architectural firm of Heins and LaFarge were the early architects and were replaced by Ralph Adams Cram in 1911. Located on Amsterdam Avenue at 112th Street, the Cathedral is in easy walking distance of the *Carl*

Schurz Monument and well worth a visit. It is the largest Gothic church in the world. We will look at the western façade with its front portals carved by John Angel with the assistance of Bruno Piccirilli. We will ignore whatever other sculptures Bruno Piccirilli may have worked on except for a frieze on the walls of The Baptistry. So enter and take in all the magnificence of this great structure.

Bruno Piccirilli (1903-1976) was the only one of the Piccirilli brothers' children to become a sculptor. He worked with John Angel (1881-1966) in Angel's Connecticut studio on the sculptures for the church and continued helping until Angel's death.

The entrance to the left of the main portal has figures of Christian martyrs with the basestone of each depicting the form of martyrdom. The figures of the entrance to the right of the main door are of theologians. The carving in the central portal has a Christ in Majesty amid seven lamps and seven stars with the evangelical symbols in the spandrels. A statue of Saint John is between the pair of doors. In the Cathedral on the walls of the Baptistry is a frieze honoring the Dutch that has been attributed to John Angel. His assistant in carving both the portal and Bapistry may have been Bruno Piccirilli.

Walk north on Amsterdam and through the campus of Columbia University at 116th Street to Low Memorial Library. Inside, in the upper part of the rotunda of Low Memorial Library there are four Piccirilli-carved statues done for Daniel

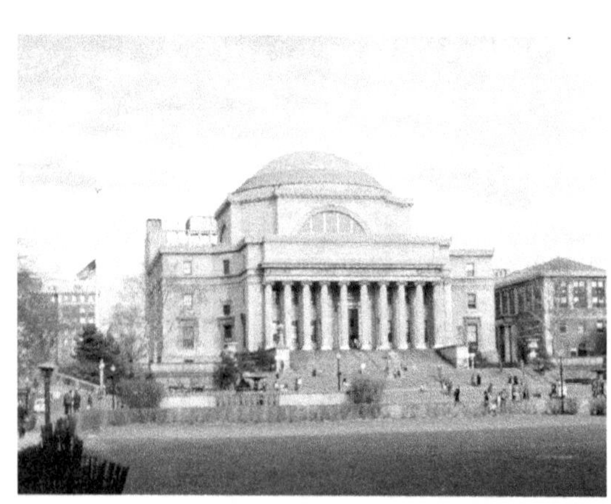

Chester French: *Euripides, Demosthenes, Caesar* and *Sophocles*. We only make mention of them, but they are easily viewed from the floor of the rotunda. Entry to the balcony level where the statues are is not allowed.

After leaving the campus head west to Riverside Drive and West 122nd Street to Mr. John D.Rockefeller Jr.'s Riverside Church. The architects were Henry C. Pelton of New York and Allen & Collens of Boston. The church began as a Baptist Church on the Lower East Side in 1841 and as Manhattan developed northward the church and Manhattan both moved along uptown several times before finally settling on this Riverside Drive site in 1930. Riverside Church, an interdenominational church, was built by John D. Rockefeller Jr. so that as many followers as possible could hear Dr. Harry Emerson Fosdick, his favorite preacher, speak. Dr. Fosdick was famous for his sermons against the beliefs of the Baptist fundamentalists, and he was in favor of a non-sectarian Christianity. He did not favor baptism by immersion and welcomed a church where Christians of any race, color, creed or denomination were welcome.[52]

In the past, purists have criticized the church for looking like Chartres Cathedral while using modern steel construction. As a result of this form of construction, certain traditional medieval building techniques, such as the use of outside buttresses, have no functional purpose and have been kept small. The efffect is to make the twenty-one-story church appear smaller than it is. Riverside Church is outstanding for its stone carving, stained glass and metal work.

Riverside Church is a Piccirilli Paradise with over 500 of their carvings in marble and wood. There is a commingling of hands in the carving of the stone sculpture of Riverside Church by the Piccirillis. The Piccirilli brothers carved the great portal, or front door, of Riverside Church with its host of statues, reliefs, gargoyles and numerous details. Bruno Piccirilli did a large share of the carving.

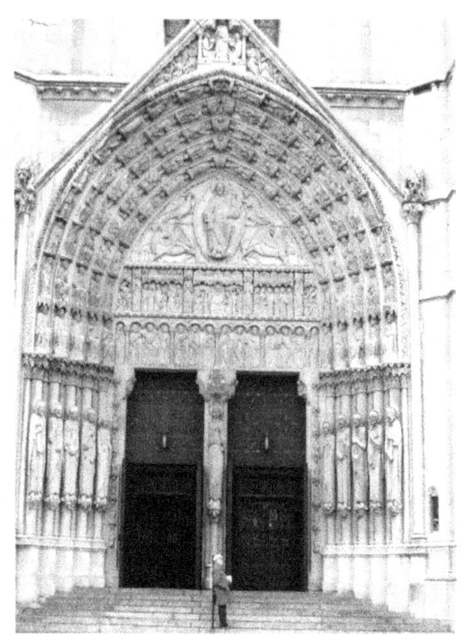

In the sculpture of the tympanum of the portal at the main entrance Jesus sits surrounded by the symbols of the Apostles Matthew, Mark, Luke and John. In the five decorative moldings (archivolts) surrounding the seated Jesus the outer ones depict angels. The middle three have forty-two statues of famous men of religion, philosophy and science and sixteen other figures as well as an arch of angels. Albert Einstein can be found at the end of the second archivolt. Alive at the time, Einstein was the only living person so honored. The sculptures of the inner three archivolts reflect the international, the interdenominational and, interracial philosophy that Riverside Church espouses.

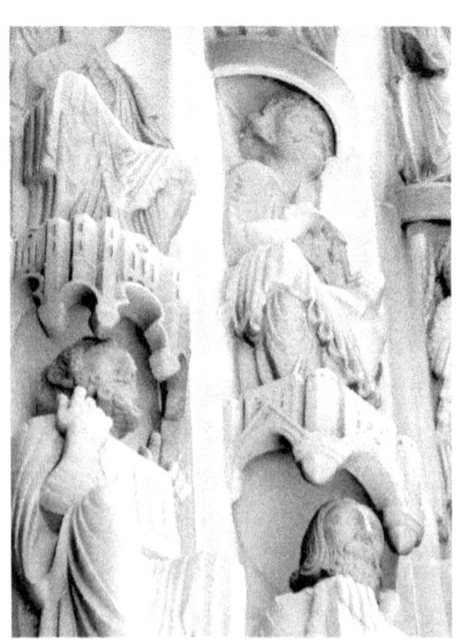

Our rough count of sculpted figures on the exterior of the church is over 340. A 1930 newspaper series about the recently opened church states that the Piccirillis "devoted three years to the monumental task of making the hundreds of statues which adorn the church. Altogether they designed 200 statues of persons, about 250 scenes carved in stone, many of them containing several figures, and nearly 150 wood carvings. And the statues "represent the greatest figures of all time—regardless of creed, color or profession."[53]

In the interior of the church, Bruno Piccirilli did the greater part of the carving for the eighty statuettes for the chancel screen along with other figurative sculptures.[54] It took Orazio Piccirilli a year and a half to design the sculpture for the

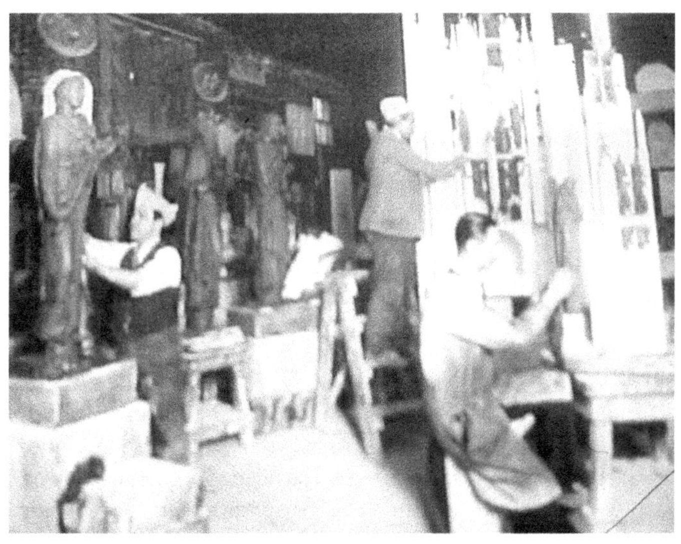

chancel screen that is divided in seven sections.[55] The sections consist of famous; Physicians, Teachers, Prophets, Humanitarians, Missionaries, Reformers and Artists. What follows is an example of a screen section and its sculptures. The sculptures that comprise the Artists' section are: *John Greenleaf Whittier, Fra Angelico, John Milton, Giovanni Palestrina, Leonardo Da Vinci*, and *Christ the Lover of Beauty* (Jesus is included in each category), *Michelangelo* and *Johann Sebastian Bach.*

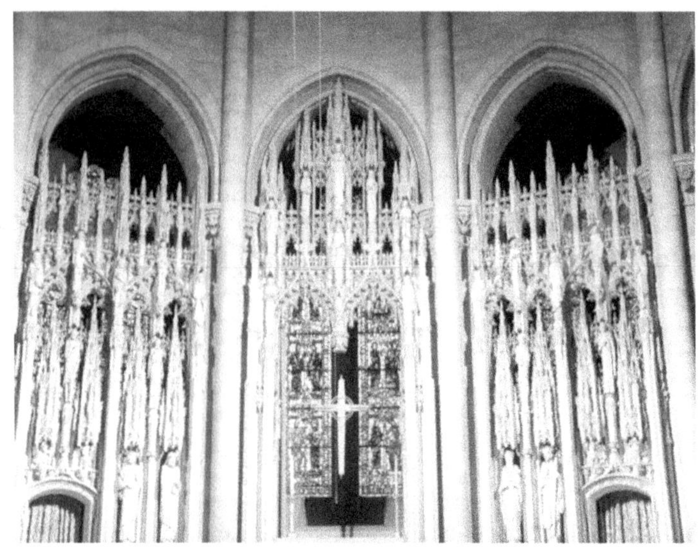

An unpublished manuscript (c.1955), by Rev. Eugene C. Corder, of the Building Committee, reveals something of the relationship between the brothers and the committee during the building of Riverside Church:

> During the construction of the church, it was often our pleasure to eat lunch with the Piccirilli group in their combination studio, workshop and home in the Bronx. They had for generations lived and worked in Italy and in New York after the manner of their craft. It was a unique experience for a group of New Yorkers to ride a subway train to the Bronx and quickly find themselves seated at a long refectory table of ancient design and construction where they would partake of a typical Italian lunch and try to rise to the demands of the jollity and good will that abounded there.[56]

There is an inexpensive portfolio of pictures for sale at the small bookshop in the Visitors' Center that might give you a closer look at the church and the mix of its sculpture. We are not finished with Riverside Church yet. Do not leave without a visit to the *Laura Spelman Rockefeller Memorial*

Carillon of 74 bells and the observation platform. Take the elevator twenty stories for the carillon and spectacular views. Be advised, however, that beyond the twentieth floor elevator stop there are one hundred and forty seven further steps. As you rise towards the heavens on foot, you might assuage your pain during the ascent in mystical contemplation of the number 147 between struggles for breath.

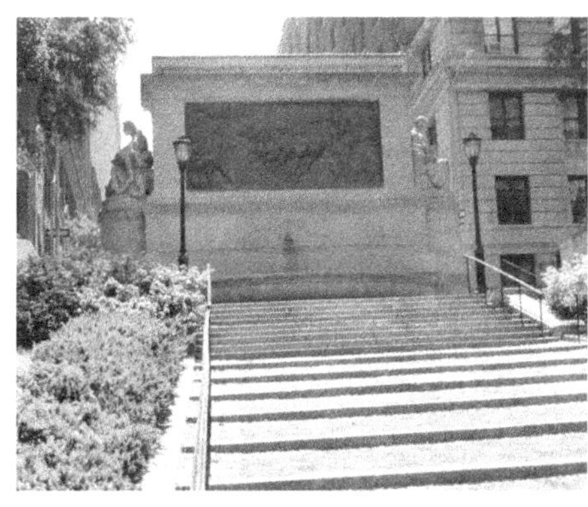

A short, twenty-two block walk might alleviate the pain of the recent Riverside ascent, or, if you prefer, don't chance walking and take a bus on Riverside Drive to the *Firemen's Memorial.* The memorial is at Riverside Drive and West 100th Street and is dedicated to the men of the New York City Fire Department who have died in the line of duty. The Fire Department has held its memorial ceremonies at this site for many years.

This memorial, which is dedicated to those who died fighting fires in, "a war that never ends," was made by Attilio Piccirilli and H. Van Buren Magonigle was the architect. The memorial was approved for construction in Union Square in1909, but its construction was delayed by objections. It was finally erected on Riverside Drive in 1913. The objections were raised by both the Fire Chief and the Parks Commissioner. The fire chief, Edward Croker, objected to the original site. He also believed that a proper monument should be a bronze statue of a fireman in working uniform so that it would be clear to everyone what the monument was all about. The parks commissioner wanted to preserve the use of

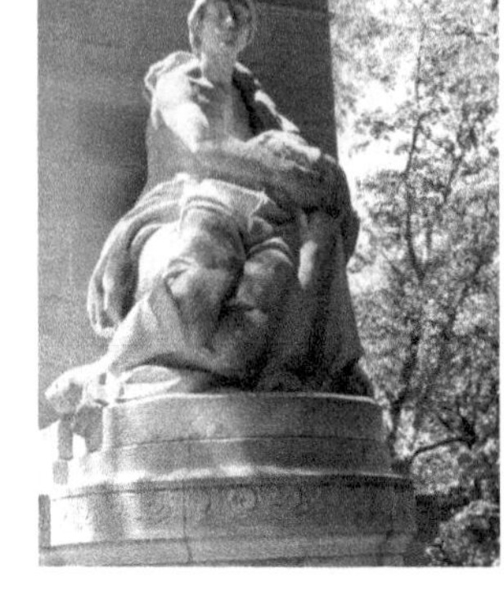

the intended site for "overwrought agitators" to continue as a place for their speech making and demonstrations.[57]

The sculpture of a woman holding a fallen firefighter in her arms stands for Sacrifice. The sculpture of a woman holding a child and a fireman's helmet represents Duty. The plaque in the ground was added by the A.S.P.C.A.in 1927 as a tribute to the fire horses of another era. We find the panel showing the horses and fire apparatus racing to the fire to be as equally attractive to us as it was to the writer of a guidebook written in 1917. It is described in the book as:

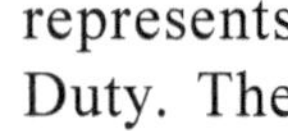

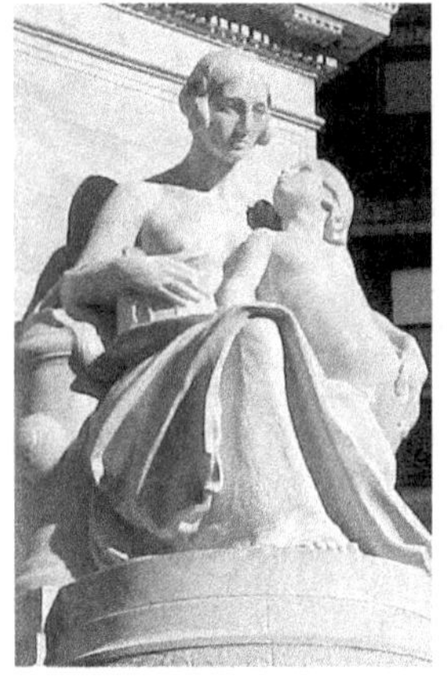

> an exquisite low relief, whose subject is 'The Call to the Fire', while at the ends are groups of 'Memory' and 'Duty.' With the passing of the fire horses, in growing favor of the motor vehicles for quick transportation of men and apparatus, we are losing a strong picturesque touch in city life, and the relief, which records the moving and stirring scene of magnificent horses straining every muscle in an effort at incredible speed while the

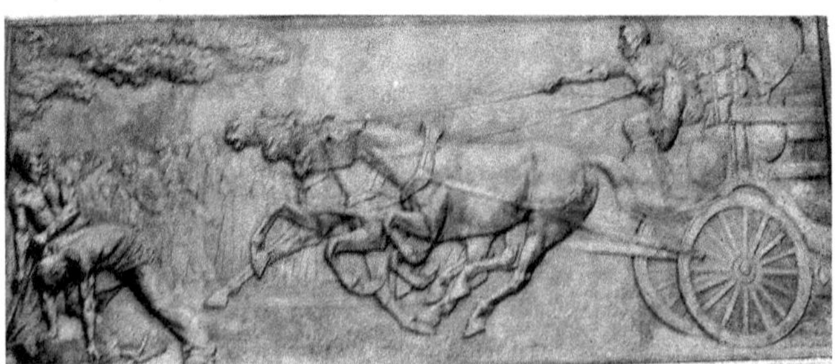

> foremen lean far over the shafts to give the fullest rein to their powers, will soon have an historic as well as an artistic interest.[58]

Earlier we saw a bronze copy of the woman holding a child, used as a grave marker at the Piccirilli grave in Woodlawn Cemetery and we will see the original of both at our next stop, *The Maine Monument.*

During a recent restoration workers found a copper box with letters by H. Van Buren Magonigle the architect of the monument and Fire Chief Edward Croker. In a 1908 fire, Chief Croker had seen his deputy fall into a blazing cellar and die. The 300 pound victim Deputy Fire Chief Charles W. Kruger fell into a flooded Canal Street basement. Though in danger themselves, three of his men made desperate attempts to save him but they could not lift him out of the water and he drowned. This experience led Chief Croker to start his campaign to build a monument to honor and remember those firemen who have died in the line of duty. A badge and firebox key belonging to the fire chief were also found in the box.[59] In 1913, the same year that the *Firemen's Memorial* was put in place, the *Maine Monument* was finally unveiled at Columbus Circle, West 59th Street and Central Park West. This is our next destination and unless you are hardier than we are, we suggest taking some form of public transportation to get to Columbus Circle. The number 5 bus that runs on Riverside Drive will get you there.

The *Maine Monument* is a memorial to the 260 men of the battleship *Maine* who died when the ship exploded in the harbor of Havana, Cuba, as well as to the others who died in the Spanish-American War. The explosion of the *Maine* had led to the start of the Spanish-American War which lasted from April 24, 1898 to December 10, 1898.

The sculpture for the *Maine Monument* was designed and carved by Attilio Piccirilli. The architect of the monument was H. Van Buren Magonigle. It was erected in 1913 after an eleven-year delay. The long delay was the result of a personality clash between publishers William Randolph Hearst and Joseph Pulitzer, as well as from Hearst's feud with the ruling Democratic boss of Tammany Hall, Charles Murphy. Problems with committees, commissions and other interested parties added to the confusion.[60]

An English visitor, a writer for the *London Evening Mail*, went to the Piccirilli studios in 1912 and reported seeing the nine pieces that form the *Maine Monument* on the studio floor. The studio floor is described as being, "like the sand of the sea, so thickly was it covered with pulverized marble"[61] —an unhealthy working environment and possibly another reason why the Piccirillis dissuaded their children from following in their footsteps. Those nine pieces are described in detail in the 1912 article, but we'll concern ourselves only with the figure of the mother comforting her child, called *Fortitude*. As mentioned before, a similar sculpture marks the grave of the Piccirilli family at Woodlawn Cemetery. Attilio called the grave marker *Mater Amorosa*. A copy of it is noted as being in the William Randolph Hearst Collection in San Simeon, California where it is called *Mater Consolatrix*.[62] We also

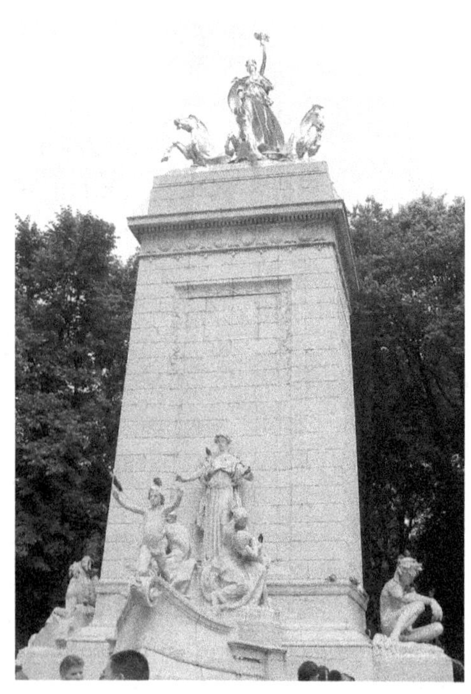

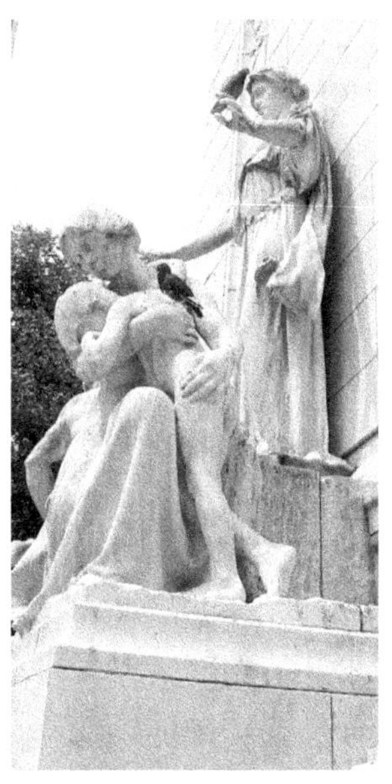

have just seen another version of the mother and child at the *Firemen's Memorial.* Piccirilli's use and reuse of the mother and child theme is thought to be because his mother and one of the Piccirilli children served as models.[63] The writer for the *London Evening Mail* describes the mother and child of the *Maine Monument* in these words, "In the grief of the mother's face, and the limp human cling of her young son's arm that encircles her neck, while he buries his face in her arm, Piccirilli has surpassed himself."[64] The same reaction is elicited today.

The gilded "Columbia Triumphant," atop the monument is supposed to have been made from cannons recovered from the battleship *Maine.*[65]

The original site selected for the *Maine Monument* was at 47th Street, where Broadway and Seventh Avenue meet. (The current location of one of the TKTS booths.) The site had been selected in 1902, but in 1906, when Attilio Piccirilli finally completed his sculptures, it was discovered that a most unusual "clerical oversight" had

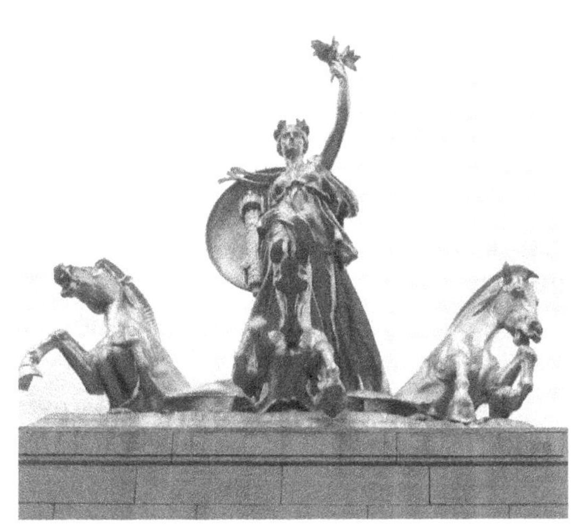

occurred. The clerk whose job it was to record the original site had not done so and it had been given over to another use. A comfort station had been built on the original site. A new site had to be found. The present one was approved in 1910 and the monument unveiled in 1913.[66]

After the *Maine Monument* had been ceremoniously unveiled it received many negative criticisms. Those criticisms, however, were offset by complimentary remarks. Most of the criticisms focussed on whether or not the monument added or detracted from the beauty of the Columbus Circle area and its effect, artistically, on the earlier built *Columbus Monument*. Recently, the architectural critic Paul Goldberger has written of the area:

> This is a chaotic jumble of streets that can be crossed in about fifty different ways—all of them wrong, not a civic square or a park corner or any of the other things it pretends to be. [After dismissing the three nearby buildings as "wretched" and providing no definition to the area, he goes on to say that the *Maine Monument*] is a pedestal that provides a firmer anchor than any of the larger buildings, and the boat containing sculptor Attilio Piccirilli's figures seems just about to sail into the center of the circle. It is a grand, if sentimental, presence which is more than can be said for the statue of Columbus, by Gaetano Russo (1892), which sits atop a column in the very center of the square, with Columbus looking as if he had been waiting since 1892 for a break in the traffic so that he might go somewhere more comfortable.[67]

We now will double back across Central Park to the East Side and stop at the Metropolitan Museum of Art where you might set aside a day or two to see the whole collection. At the Met we can get a close-up and more intimate view of the Piccirilli genius. The main entrance to the museum is on Fifth Avenue at 82rd Street. There is an admission charge which leaves it up to you how much of the "suggested" admission you wish to pay. While in the museum it is strongly recommended that you see everything that you can. Keep in mind that the admission button also is good for the Cloisters, way uptown.

We go directly to the American Wing and the Charles Engelhard Court. On the wall to your right are two relief portraits in marble, *The Children of Prescott Hall Butler* and *The Children of Jacob H. Schiff.* Both were carved by the Piccirilli Brothers Studio from the original bronzes of Augustus Saint-Gaudens. Prescott Hall Butler was a distinguished lawyer and brother-in-law of Stanford White. Jacob H. Schiff was a prominent New York banker and philanthropist. A placard near the Butler relief says, "Most American sculptors working in the late nineteenth and early twentieth centuries employed the Piccirillis to execute many of their works in marble, a tribute to their skill and reliability as stonecutters."[68]

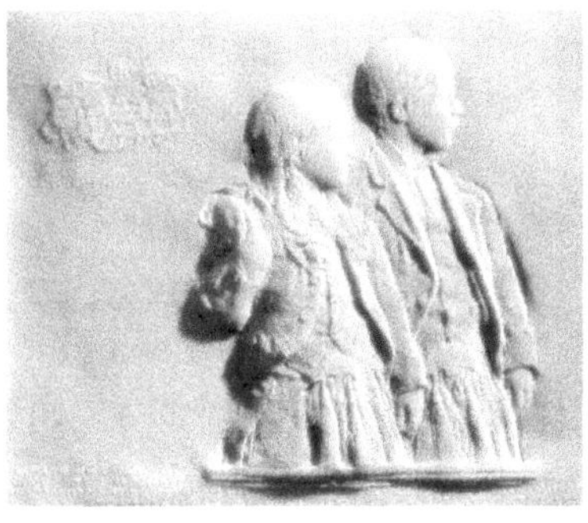

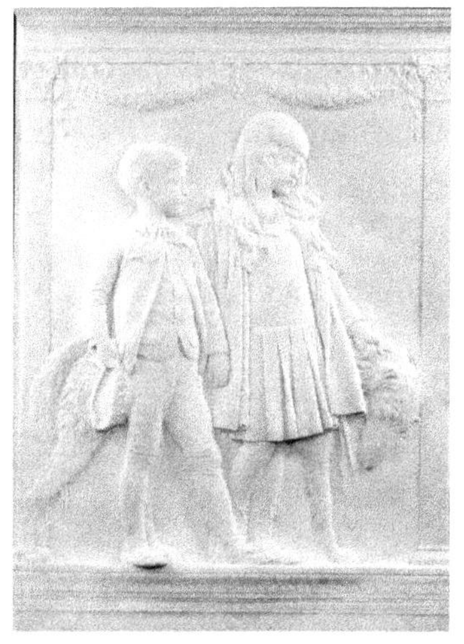

Across the courtyard is *Memory*, by Daniel Chester French. French considered it his best piece. It shows the Muse of Memory holding a mirror reflecting upon the ephemeral nature of youth, beauty and life. *Memory* was carved by the Piccirilli brothers.

On the balcony overlooking the courtyard is *The Angel of Death and the Sculptor* also known as *The Milmore Memo-*

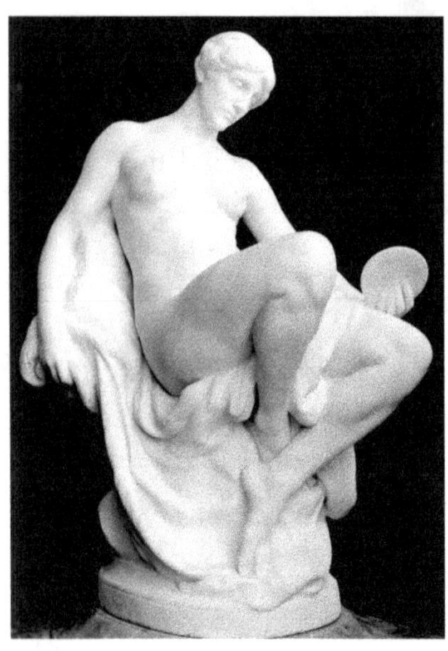

rial, also by French and a masterpiece. It depicts Death interrupting the sculptor Martin Milmore (1844-1883) as he carves a sphinx that he was commissioned to make for a memorial to the Union soldiers who died in the Civil War. The original is in Forest Hills Cemetery, Jamaica Hills, Massachusetts and marks the Milmore family plot.[69] Around 1869 Martin Milmore created the Civil War memorial statue replicas of which can be found in a great number of American cities. The statue is of a Union soldier, "standing, leaning on his rifle, contemplating the grave of his fallen comrades."[70] Nearby, on the balcony, is *Mourning Victory,* another D.C. French masterpiece. The original honors three brothers from the Melvin family who died in the Civil War and is in Sleepy Hollow Cemetery in

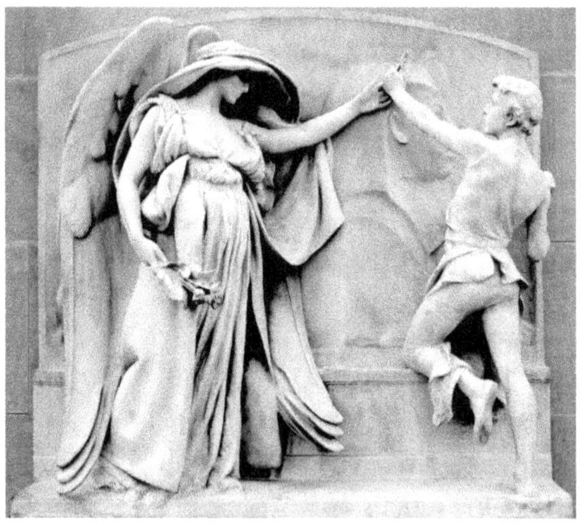

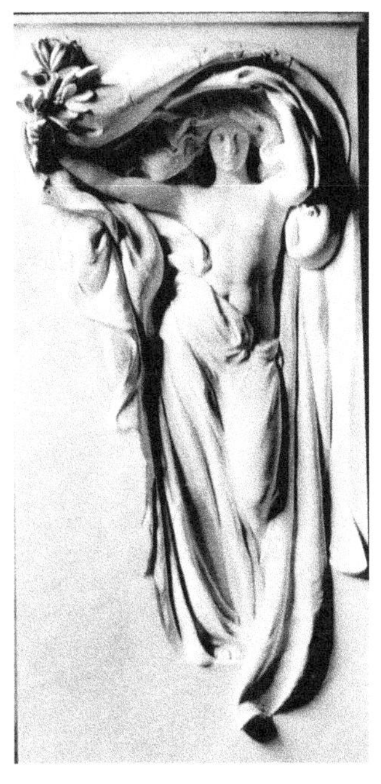

Concord, Massachusetts where it is part of *The Melvin Memorial*.[71] Both memorials were carved by the Piccirillis.

Ask a guard to direct you to the Henry R. Luce Study Center and go to Study Case 109Q. The Luce Center provides a large collection of American art for further study. Acquisition number 26.113 (The 113th object acquired by the Met in 1926) marks the white marble nude figure of Attilio Piccirilli's *Fragelina*. In its day *Fragelina* was one of his most popular pieces, but here it is consigned to virtual oblivion by changing taste. Number 19.185, *Study of a Head*, is also by Attilio and 29.13, is Furio Piccirilli's black marble sculpture, *Seal*. Play a computer for more information.

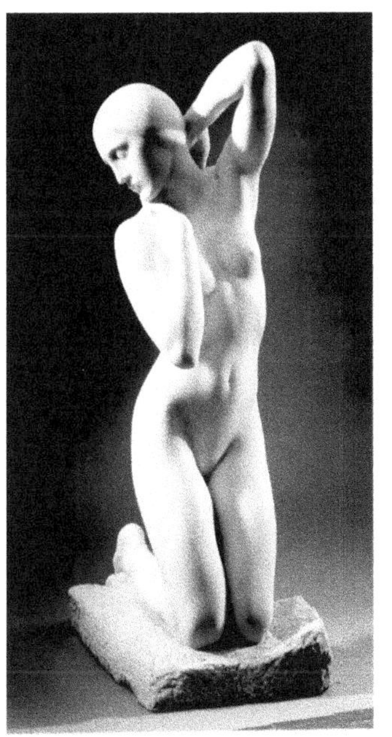

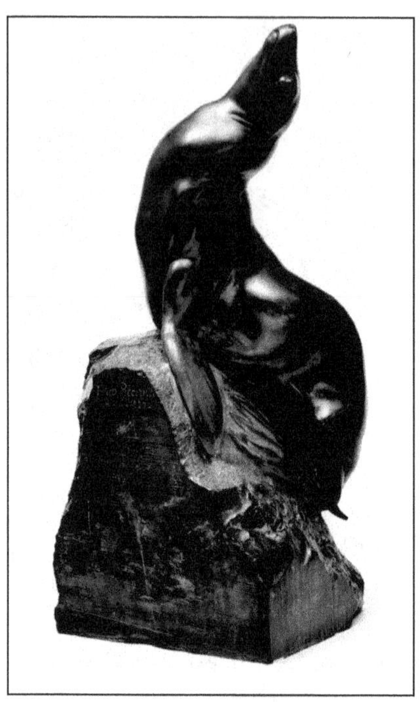

Move on; move on down the road to Fifth Avenue and East 70th Street to the former home of Henry Clay Frick (1849-1919) which now houses the Frick Collection.

Henry Clay Frick made his money in the steel industry and to many historians he was one of the less savory characters in American industrial history. He was president of Carnegie Steel Company. In June 1892 his unionized steelworkers in Homestead, Pennsylvania threatened to strike

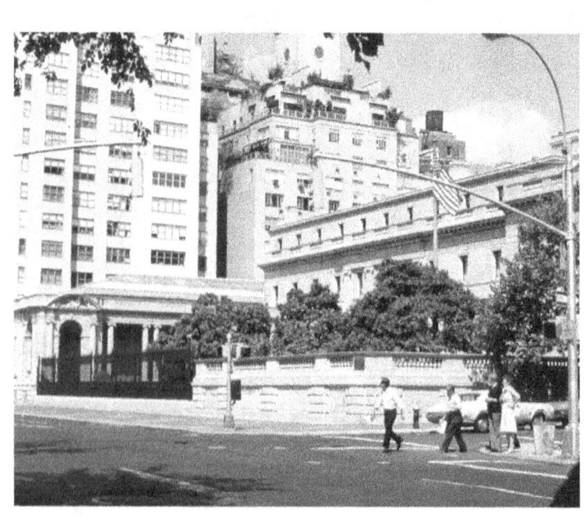

after Frick had cut their wages and locked them out. Frick attempted to replace the unionized workers with non-union men. In July he hired 300 armed Pinkerton detectives to protect the replacement workers from the angry strikers. The Pinkerton Detective Agency was no stranger to labor disputes having been involved in about seventy of them. When the Pinkertons arrived at Homestead aboard two barges, the angry steelworkers used guns, dynamite and even a cannon to keep them from coming ashore. In the ensuing battle three workers and seven Pinkertons were killed with many more injured. After the Pinkertons surrendered they were brutally beaten by the workers. Public sympathy, which had favored the workers, was changed by this action and was further eroded when an assassin attempted to kill Frick. Frick asked and received from the governor of Pennsylvania National Guardsmen to restore order. 8,500 troops were sent, the strike broken and the mill went back into production using 1,700 replacement workers.[72]

The Frick Mansion, designed by the architects Carrere and Hastings, dates from 1914. The mansion became a public museum in 1935 and occupies part of the site of a farm owned by Robert Lenox on land he purchased prior to 1829. His son, James Lenox, a bibliophile, inherited the land and built the Lenox Library. The Lenox Library was designed by the architect Richard Morris Hunt whose memorial by Daniel Chester French (1898) is on Fifth Avenue, across from the museum. When the Lenox Library was torn down to make way for the Frick Mansion the 85,000 book collection was given to the New York Public Library and still forms a part of the Astor, Lenox and Tilden Collections at the main branch on 42nd Street.

On the East 71st Street side of the Frick Museum *Orpheus*, by Attilio Piccirilli, is easily identifiable by the lyre he holds. Further East on 71st Street, closer to the Frick Library is *Sculpture* another bas relief by Attilio this time of a female

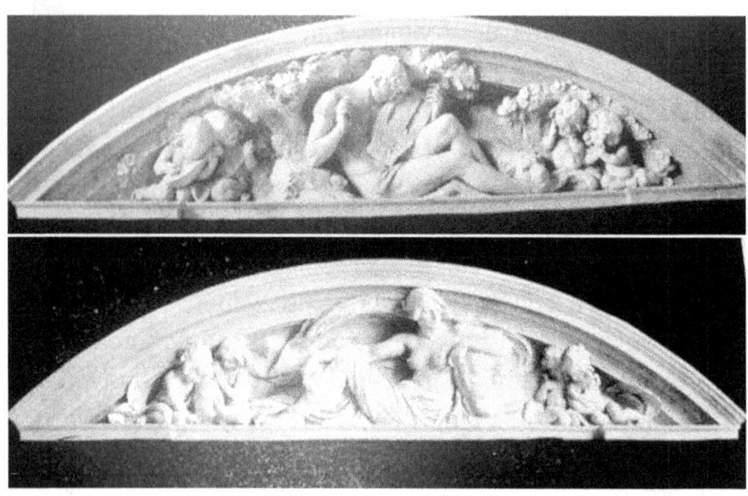

figure holding a sculptor's mallet. The 70th Street entrance to the Frick has what looks like a Piccirilli sculpture over the doorway but it is by Sherry E. Fry. Go into the Frick. The museum has a marvelous collection and offers a view of life lived on another level. Turn left at the ticket taker and enter the hallway whose vaulted ceiling is covered with marble. Orazio Piccirilli did all the carvings on the ceiling. On the panels in the room and between the panels are carved pastoral scenes by Orazio. Off to the left and right of the hallway are marble doorways he designed and decorated with all manner of vegetal matter: oak, laurel, fruit; all in Renaissance style.[73]

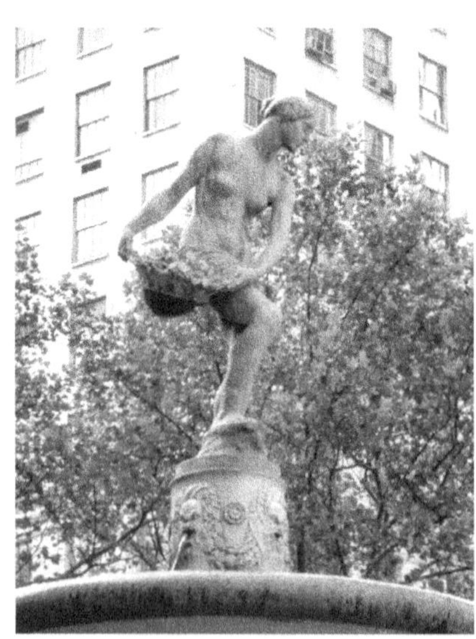

Put on your running shoes for the fourteen-block jog to, and a short stop at, the *Pulitzer Memorial Fountain* (1916) in

Grand Army Plaza at Fifth Avenue and 58th Street. Across 59th Street is a second plaza with Augustus Saint-Gaudens'equestrian statue of Civil War General William Tecumseh Sherman.

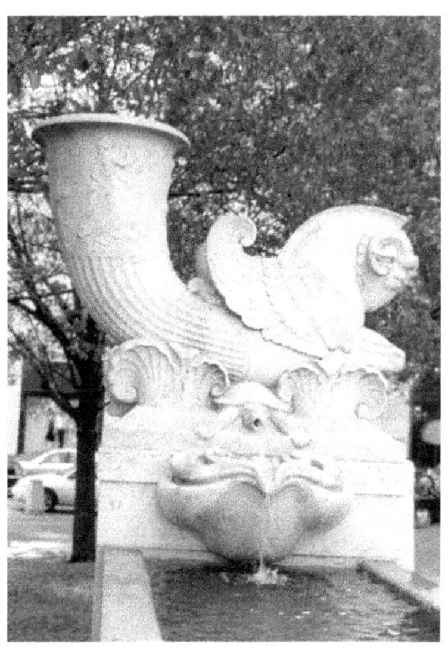

Carrere and Hastings designed the *Pulitzer Memorial Fountain* which is also known as the *Fountain of Abundance.* The figure of *Pomona,* forms a central part of the fountain. She is the goddess of Abundance and holds a basket of fruit that announces that theme. The statue is by Karl Bitter who in 1898 had proposed a second fountain for the plaza where the *Sherman Monument* now stands.[74] The two marble cornucopias were carved by Orazio Piccirilli and continue the theme of abundance.

Trot on down to Rockefeller Center that "island of architectural excellence,"[75] where the sculptural style is best described as modern classicism. Proceed to 636 Fifth Avenue between, 50th and 51st Streets where Attilio Piccirilli's bas-relief *Youth Leading Industry* is over the entrance. The relief is made up of numerous blocks of cast glass— an early use of this medium— and can be illuminated at night.[76] The heraldic device above the sculpture is also by Attilio. Walk down Fifth Avenue to15 West 48th Street where there is a handsome bas-relief titled, *The Joy of Life*, over the doorway. The colorful composition shows a reclining Bacchus with standing figures on each side of him; a tame orgy. It too is by Attilio Piccirilli.

In Rockefeller Center you can find sculpture by many of the fine artists of the 1930's. Quite a few of the sculptures

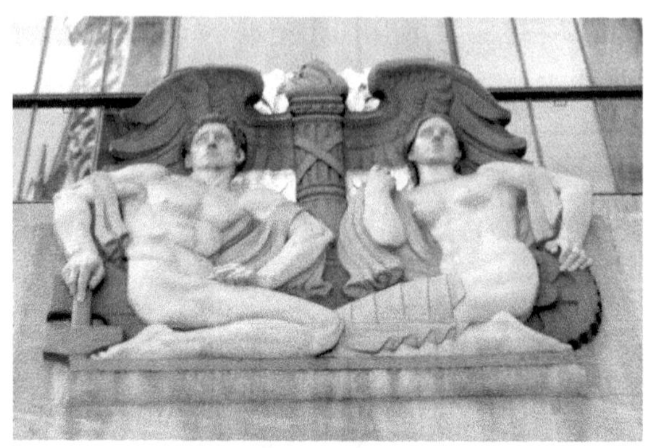

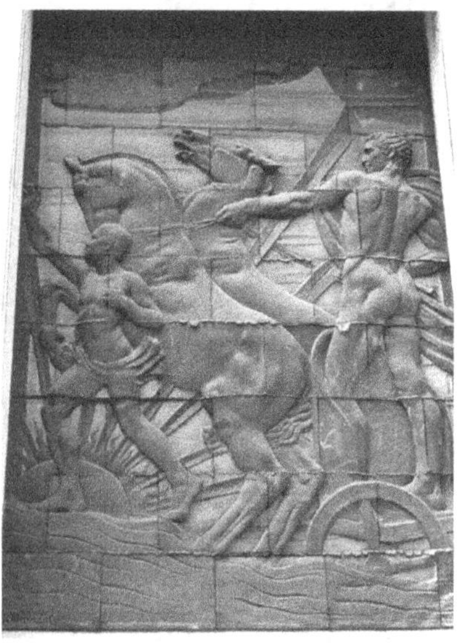

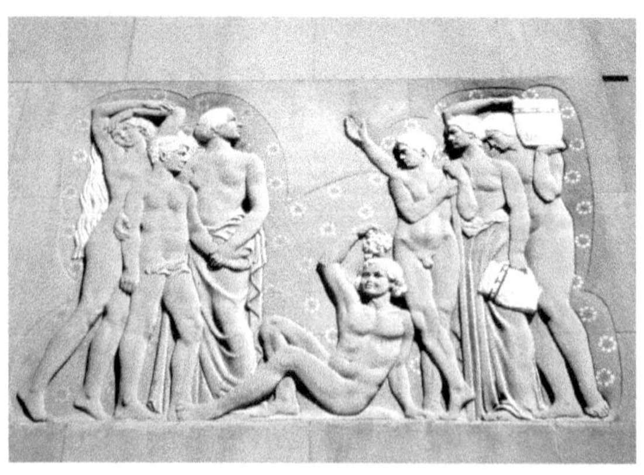

were carved by the Piccirilli Brothers Marble Carving Studio. The Piccirilli Brothers carved the stone relief of the *British Coat of Arms for Carl Paul Jennewein* which is above the 620 5th Avenue entrance to the British Empire Building. The sculptor, Leo Lentelli designed the spandrels at the top of 626 5th Avenue (*Four Periods in Italian History*) and 636 5th Avenue (*Four Continents*) buildings. The designs were carried out by the Piccirilli brothers. Alfred Janniot's relief sculpture *Gallic Freedom* which is above the entrance to 610 5th Avenue was another carved by the brothers. Lee Lawrie, whose bronze *Atlas* on 5th Avenue is a favorite of photographers, did other major works at Rockefeller Center. Other sculptures by Lee Lawrie which were carved by the Piccirilli Brothers are: *Story of Mankind* (29 W. 50th St.); *World Peace* (above 50th St. entrance); *Progress* (above 49th St. entrance) and the glass and stone reliefs, *Wisdom , Sound and Light* (30 Rockefeller Plaza).[77]

Head easterly over to Saint Bartholomew's Church located on Park Avenue between East 50th and 51st Streets. The architect of the church, opened in 1918, was Bertram G. Goodhue. The present church structure replaces the original St. Bartholomew that was located at Madison Avenue and 44th Street. The portal, along with many other parts, came from the old church on Madison Avenue.[78]

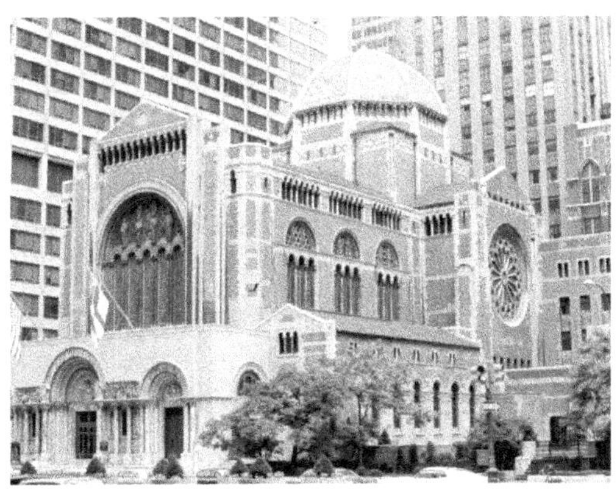

Enter the church through any of its three doors and you will be in the narthex, a sort of long hall. The mosaics on the

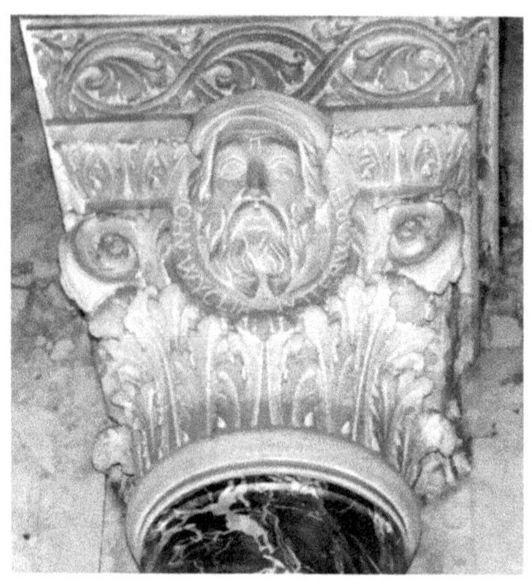

ceiling are by Hildreth Meiere and show the Creation. Buy the inexpensive pamphlet, *Saint Bartholomew's Church in the City of New York* from the shop in the narthex for a near complete and succinct description of the interior and exterior of the church. Each capital on the columns in the narthex has a carved head. The head is of "exemplary Christians...each of whom has made a significant contribution to ecclesiastical or humanitarian work."[79] The Piccirillis carved the capitals and the pamphlet will explain and describe them. Similarly described are the twin columns that line the aisles of the church and chapel. Stand facing the altar in the church; the columns on the left side portray scenes from the Old Testament; those on the right aisle have scenes from the New Testament. This arrangement follows medieval tradition.[80] The carvings on the capitals of the columns in the church and the altar are by the Piccirillis.

The involvement of the Piccirillis with the sculptural program at St. Bartholomew's is put succinctly by Christine Smith:

> Most of the architectural sculpture was executed, with varying degrees of success, by the Piccirilli Brothers firm, and much of it is cast stone rather than natural stone. The architectural sculpture includes the figures on the west façade and the south transept; the capitals in the narthex, church, and chapel; the reliefs on the north transept of the church and south flank of the chapel; the tracery for all the windows; and the narrative relief panels in the crossing.[81]

View them all, pamphlet in hand.

The next stop is 42nd Street and Fifth Avenue and the Central Research Branch of the New York Public Library or as it is now called, Humanities and Social Science. The building was completed in 1911; the architects were Carrere and Hastings. Above the main entrance between six statues—that we will get to later— are three carved panels. They are headed: "The Astor Library," "The Lenox Library" and "The Tilden Trust." John Jacob Astor, who made his fortune in furs, shipping, and real estate, collected books in his later years. James Lenox, as previously noted in the entry for the Frick Museum, was a bibliophile. The private libraries of James Lenox and John Jacob Astor formed an early part of the New York Public Library's holdings, as did 15,000 books from Samuel J. Tilden, a lawyer and politician. In his will Tilden bequeathed 15,000 books and $5,000,000 (reduced to $2,000,000 by squabbling relatives) to build a free public library.[82] The library, after some difficulties, was built on the site of a former reservoir and completed in 1911 after ten years of construction.

Guarding the entrance are the very popular couchant lions. They are popularly known as Patience and Fortitude, (a

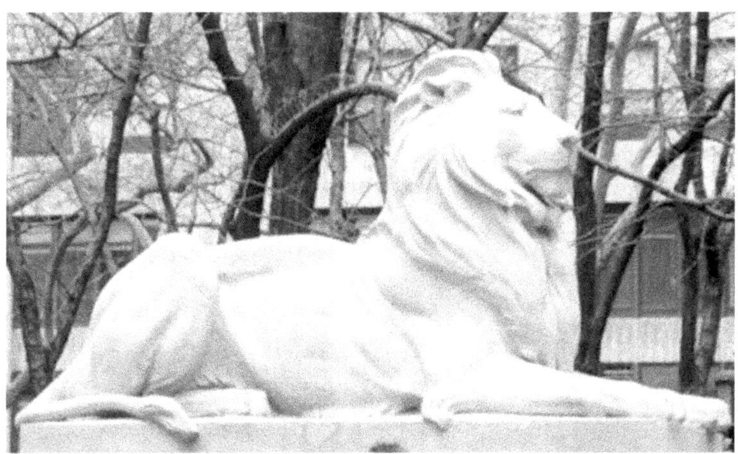

LaGuardia motto and useful qualities for living in this city and for anyone doing research and using microfilm). The marble lions are by Edward Clark Potter (1857-1923) and were carved by the Piccirilli brothers.

The six statues above the entrance, each eleven feet tall, separating the Astor, Lenox and Tilden panels, are representations of History, Drama, Poetry, Religion, Romance and Philosophy. The statues are by Paul Wayland Bartlett (1865-1925). The Piccirilli brothers carved them.

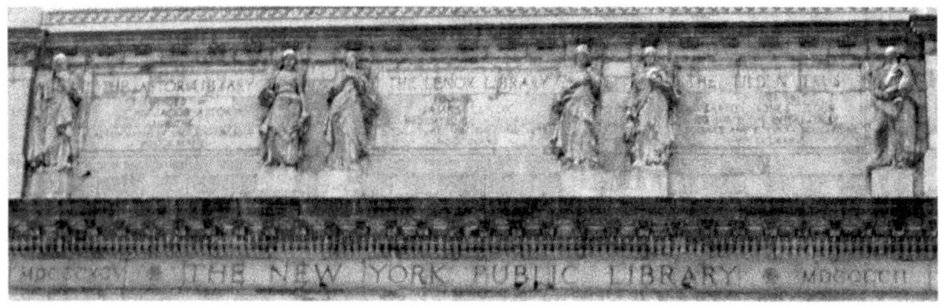

Walk up the steps between lions and examine the marvelous flagpole bases, the fountains on either side of the entrance and ascend the steps flanked by the two large urns. Glance, if you will, at the six statues above as you pass through this, "imperial entrance to the people's palace."[83] Take a tour of the library and examine the wealth of detail and beautifully crafted objects of various materials. Free tours are given. For information call (212) 930-0830 or visit www.nypl.org.

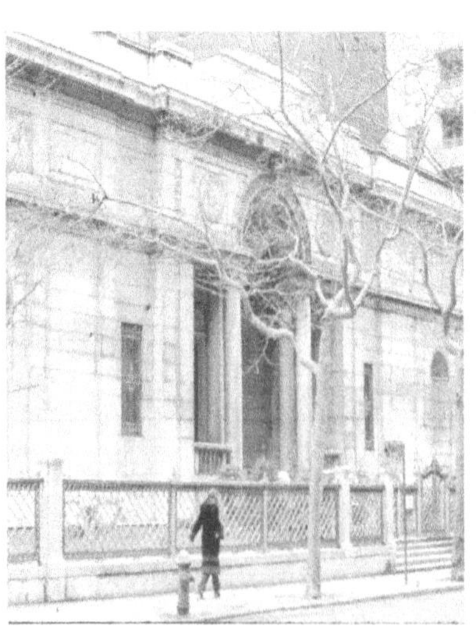

A short walk from the New York Public Library is the Pierpont Morgan Library at 33 East 36th Street. It was designed by McKim,

Mead and White and completed in 1906. Its construction is unusual as its outer facing of marble is put together without the use of mortar; a method used in classical antiquity. The simplicity of the exterior of the Morgan Library belies the grandeur within. The six mural medallions are by Attilio Piccirilli. The Morgan houses an outstanding collection of rare books, prints and manuscripts, among other treasures.

Our next destination is Greenwich Village in general, Washington Square Park in particular, and, specifically, the Washington Arch at the foot of Fifth Avenue, another Piccirilli Brothers project. The present marble arch replaces a wooden one that had been erected in 1889 for the centennial of George Washington's first inauguration. Designed by Stanford White in 1892 the present arch was completed in 1895. A writer on city art had this to say about the arch in 1917:

> The arch is one of those carefully transplanted bits of foreign architecture by which one soon learns in New York, to recognize the hand of Stanford White. Very perfect and charming in themselves, they have no special relevancy to the city, nor to the purpose to which they have been adapted, and stand in time and character as so many exotics in a provincial setting.[84]

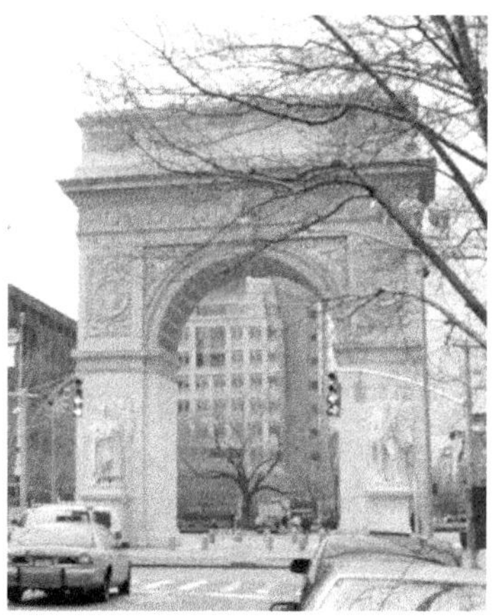

The original designs for the figures of Washington were by Frederick MacMonnies and "were enthusiastically approved"[85] by Stanford White. Many delays necessitated a change of plans and sculptor (among them the 1906 murder of Stanford White by Harry Thaw). It wasn't until 1918 that the last sculpture was finished and put in place. The left figure is of Washington as Commander in Chief flanked by "Fame"

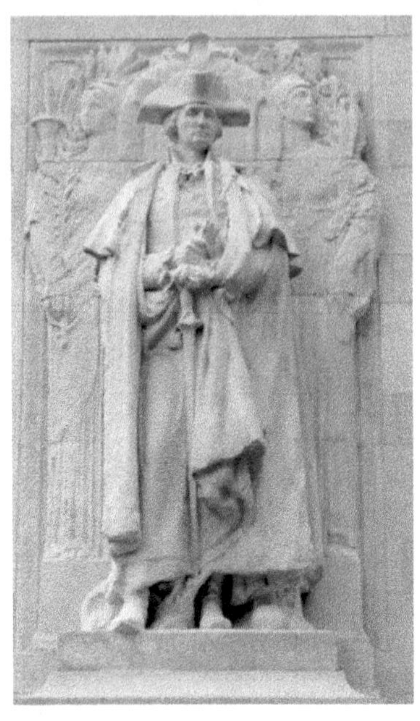

and "Valor." It is by Hermon MacNeil (1916). The figure of Washington as a statesman with "Justice" and "Wisdom," on the west pier, is by Alexander Stirling Calder (1918), father of Alexander Calder. The eagle is by Philip Martiny. The Piccirilli brothers did most of the sculptural carving for the arch that recently has undergone restoration.

Washington Square Park is built on what was originally marshland with Minetta Brook, still actively flowing below ground, running through it. The marsh became a burying ground in 1797 and a hanging ground that drew large crowds on execution days. In 1823 the burial ground was leveled and filled in. It was abandoned until about 1827 when it became the Washington Parade Ground. It next became a park with plantings and walks surrounded by a fence. The reconstructed area then attracted the wealthy who built their homes along the edges of the park. Some of the mansions still remain.

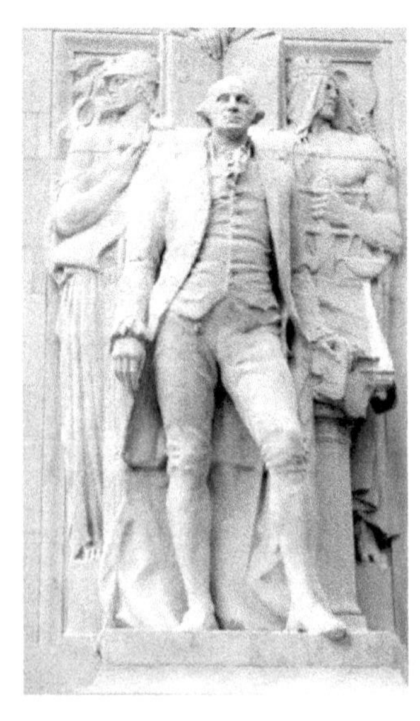

For more of the history of Greenwich Village, circa 1633, Helen Henderson had this to say:

> the Dutch records make reference to the Indian Village of *Sappokanican*, where Hudson is supposed to have stopped for supplies, and identified as lying east of the Gansevoort Market ...Wouter Van Twiller, the second Dutch governor, is the earliest connected with the Greenwich Village. Amongst other prerequisites of his governorship, this astute Dutchman appropriated to himself the Company Farm, No. 3 ...to be adapted by Providence to the setting of his own private tobacco plantation. His farmhouse probably the first on the island to be erected beyond the protective limit of the fort, marked the founding of the *Bossen Bouwerie*, or farm in the woods, by which *Sappokanican* came to be known in the Dutch language. The English called it Greenwich.[86]

This next stop for the devoted Piccirilli fan involves a walk from the far west of Greenwich Village and the *Bossen Bouwerie* of Wouter van Twiller to the far east of the East Village to see the first location of the Leonardo Da Vinci Art School. It was located on the site of Peter Stuyvesant's *Bouwerie,* which he had bought in 1651. "Here he [Peter Stuyvesant] built a manor and a chapel. Here he would live out his life and be buried, and here, over the parade of centuries, the flappers, shtetl refugees, hippies and punks—an aggregate of local residents running from Trotsky to Auden to Charlie Parker to Joey Ramone—would shuffle past his tomb."[87]

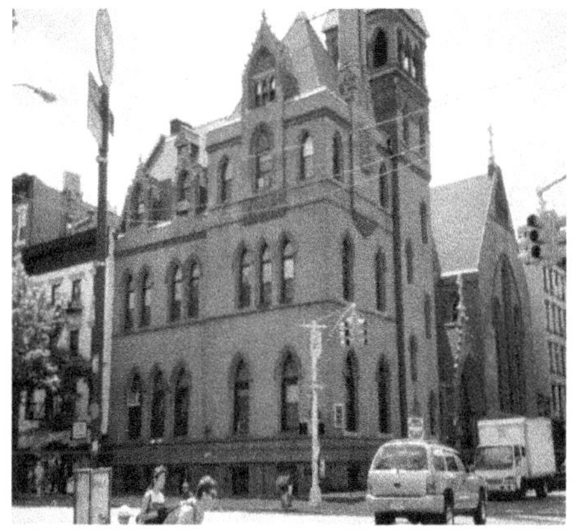

The Leonardo Da Vinci Art School was formally opened in 1923 and was founded by Onorio Ruotolo, Attilio Piccirilli and friends (all members of the Italian-American Art Association). The use of Saint Mark's Chapel at 288 East 10th

Street and Avenue A was offered by Saint Mark's in-the-Bowery Church and the school functioned at various sites until 1940. Isamu Noguchi attended the Leonardo Da Vinci Art School where, encouraged by the then director Onorio Ruotolo, he made up his mind to become a sculptor.[88] Saint Mark's Chapel (1883) still stands looking as it has always looked. It is now Saint Nicholas Carpatho Russian Orthodox Greek Catholic Church. The church and the area are worth investigating.

Before reaching our next stopover, the Civic Center, you might get something to eat in nearby Chinatown, a great favorite of ours for good and inexpensive food. Beside the great number of Chinese restaurants there are places for Malaysian, Thai, Vietnamese, Korean and Japanese food as well.

Proceed to 60 Centre Street, to the New York County Courthouse whose columns are topped by the largest capitals ever made in America. The capitals are solid granite eight feet six inches high and were done by Piccirilli brothers in classical Greek style.[89] The interior of this building with its murals, other sculpture and displays is well worth the hassle of going through their security procedures to enter.

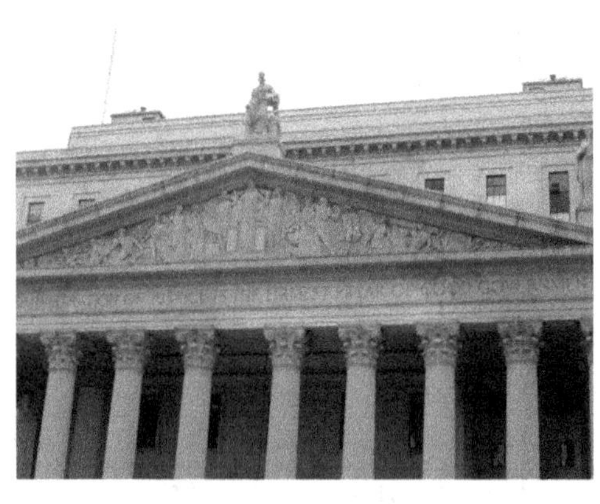

A few blocks south at Police Plaza is the New York City Police Headquarters. Entering the building you will find a rather large, shiny bronze monument completed in 1940 by Attilio Piccirilli. The statue depicts a police officer and a young boy. It is known as *The Police Memorial Statue*. The models

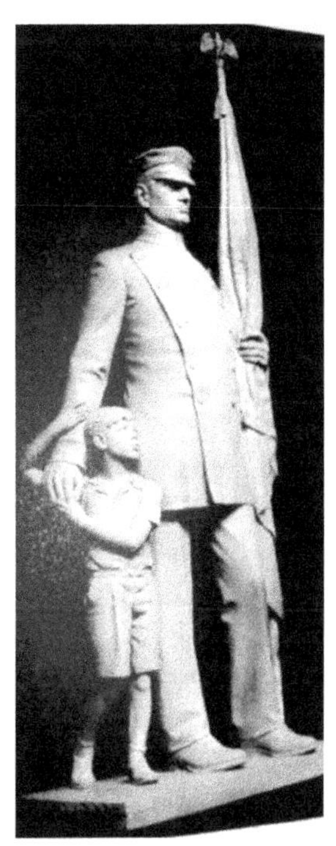

were Patrolman Martin Gillen and Eric LaGuardia the then nine year old son of Mayor LaGuardia. Attilio also made, (though it's not on display), the *Police Department Medal for Valor* that is the Department's third highest award. The medal has an image of the *Police Memorial Statue* at its center and is awarded for acts of personal bravery.[90]

The New York Stock Exchange is an easy walk from Police Headquarters. Follow Broadway to Wall Street with its interesting history, sculpture and architecture. Go into a few buildings. We especially recommend the Woolworth Building, the Trinity Building, the churches and, most especially, 1 Wall Street. Enter the Wall Street lobby [In this age of fear and security it may no longer be possible] of this branch of the Bank of New York, and be dazzled by the art deco mosaics of Hildreth Meiere (1892-1961). Continue down Wall Street to Broad Street which in Dutch colonial days was a canal for drainage and shipping, and on your right you will find the New York Stock Exchange (1903) by George B. Post. Gaze ye upward at the pediment of this classical style building and look upon the work of a young

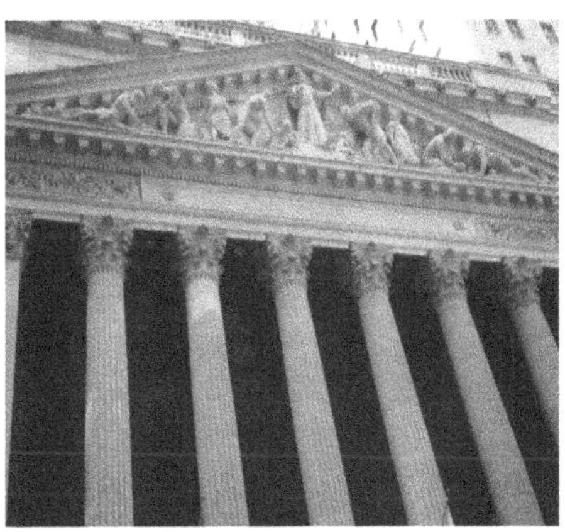

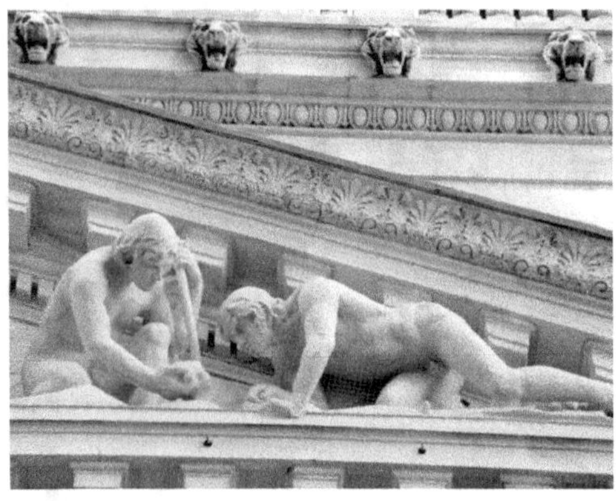

Getulio Piccirilli. Well, not upon the original work, but a zinc-coated copper replacement for the decayed original. Getulio was only eighteen years old when he was given the job of carving this pediment that goes by the name of *Integrity Protecting the Works of Man.* John Quincy Adams Ward (1830-1910), the designer of the pediment, was one of the leading sculptors in the second half of the nineteenth century. There are many sculptures by Ward around the city. A notable one is nearby; that of George Washington on the steps of Federal Hall National Memorial. Central Park has three Ward statues that you may be familiar with: *The Indian Hunter* (1866), *William Shakespeare* (1870) and *The Pilgrim* (1884).

Ward was seventy-one years old and busy with other commissions when he undertook the pedimental sculpture on the Stock Exchange. His assistant, Paul Wayland Bartlett, (you've heard of him before in reference to the six attic figures above the entrance to the New York Public Library), modeled the figures and Getulio Piccirilli "enlarged the models to the proper scale and executed all the actual stone cutting."[91]

Just a hoot and a holler away at the foot of Broadway by Bowling Green is our final Piccirilli stop in Manhattan, the United States Custom House. The Custom House (1907) by Cass Gilbert is one of New York City's outstanding buildings inside and out. It stands on the site of Fort Amsterdam built in 1626 by the early Dutch settlers.

Fort Amsterdam was erected at what was then the tip of Manhattan Island. Water was behind it and present Pearl Street was then the East River boundary. Greenwich Street was the shoreline's limits to the west. All the land presently beyond these boundaries is landfill. After a few changes of hands and names it became Fort George under the English. Fort George was razed in 1789 to be replaced by Government House which was meant to be George Washington's executive mansion; but the government moved to Philadelphia. The site underwent several more changes until the present structure was built in 1907.

The United States Custom House, now the home of The National Museum of the American Indian was used to collect custom duties on foreign imports from ships entering the nation's most important port of entry. Before the institution of the income tax the government's major source of income came from this custom tax. The desk in the rotunda at which the custom collectors worked remains and is a landmark. Above is a mural by Reginald Marsh showing in progressive panels the arrival of an ocean liner into the harbor to its docking. The marble carvings in the room, mostly with maritime motifs, are by Masaniello and Ferruccio Piccirilli.[92] Their father, Guiseppe, also worked on the Custom House.

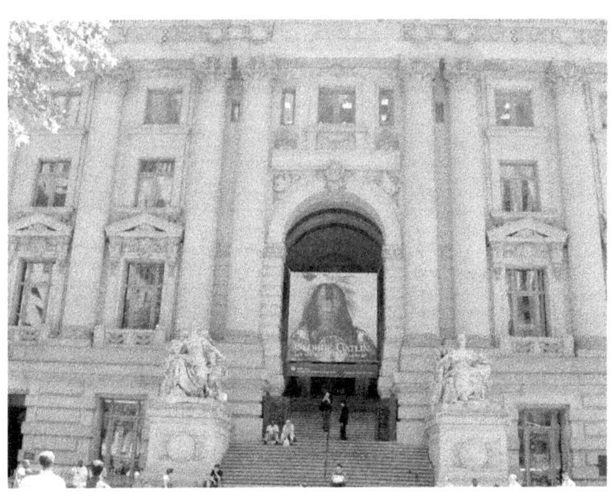

Outside the building, at the top, are twelve statues each representing a great commercial center of the world. From left to right they are: *Greece* and *Rome* by Frank Ewell, *Phoencia* by Frederick Wellington Ruckstall, *Genoa* by August Lukeman, *Venice* and *Spain* by Francois Tonetti, *Holland* and *Portugal* by Louis St. Gaudens, *Denmark* by Johannes Gerlert, and *Belgium*, *France* and *England* by Charles Grafly. *Belgium* started out as *Germany* before World

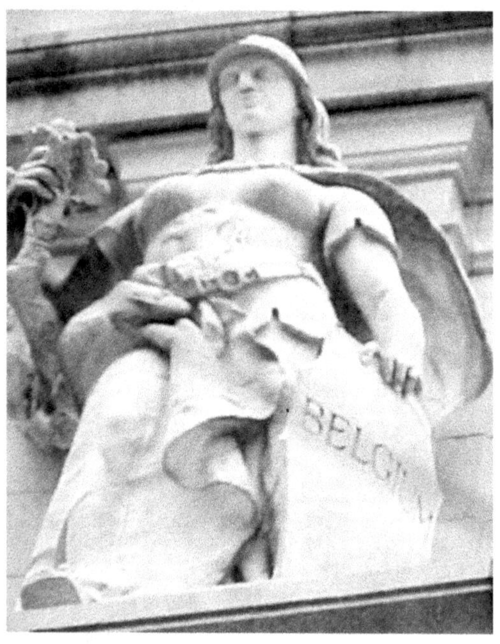

War I. Anti-German sentiment was so strong because of the war that it was felt that something had to be done to avoid trouble. Attilio Piccirilli made alterations to the statue of *Germany* and transformed it into *Belgium.* Though some of the sculptures might have been carved by the Piccirillis, the contract each sculptor signed made each sculptor responsible for executing both the models and the carving.[93]

Seated on pedestals in the front of the Custom House are figures representing the *Four Continents* (1903-1907) by Daniel Chester French, assisted by Adolph Weinman. All four

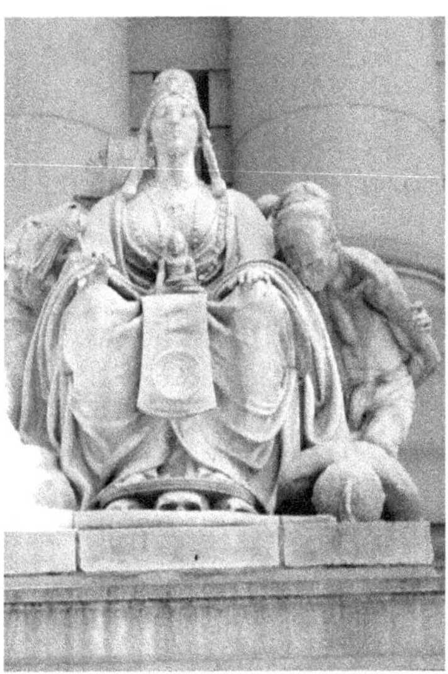

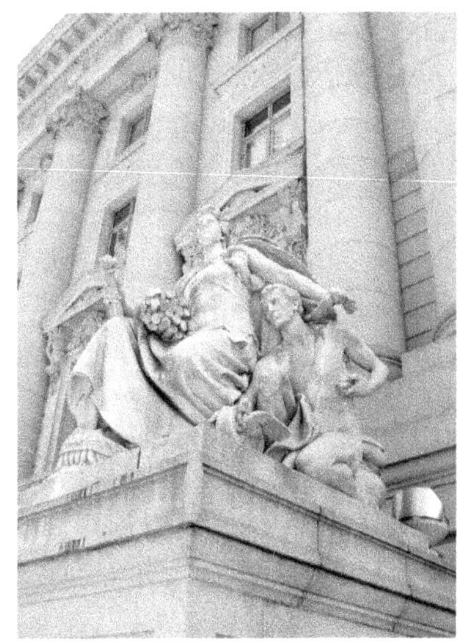

limestone sculptures were carved by the Piccirilli brothers. They are, left to right, *Asia, America, Europe* and *Africa.* The chauvinism and stereotypes the sculptures reflect are the beliefs of the doctrine of Manifest Destiny that were still prevalent and still strong.[94] The ideas of Manifest Destiny are evident in the explanation of their symbolism as given by the building's architect Cass Gilbert. Gilbert described *Asia*

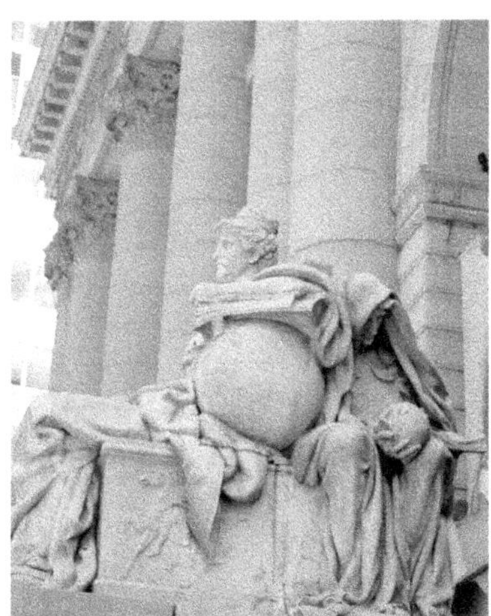

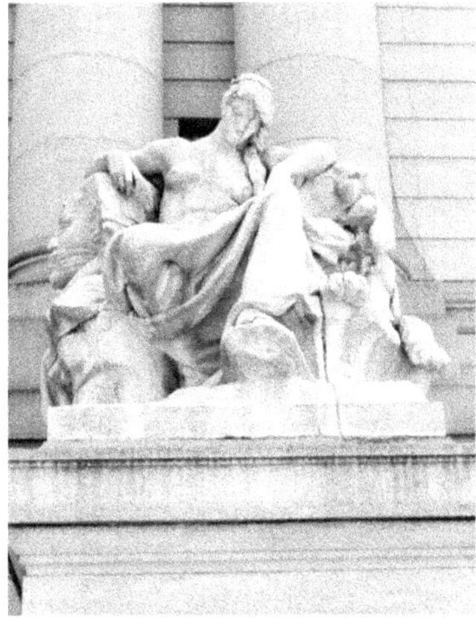

as, "calm and serene in itself…the face impassive." And in the group to her left are, "toiling prostrate figures representing the masses of humanity borne down by superstition, tyranny and oppression." *America* is a "beautiful, alert, young female figure, rising to meet new conditions of civilization, eager for advancement in all that makes peace and happiness." *Europe* is, "an Imperial figure of the highest intelligence" and *Africa*, asleep, has behind her, "a heavily draped and cowled figure, mystical, veiled, contemplative and impenetrable."[95] How's them onions baby!

You might try walking across the Brooklyn Bridge from Manhattan for a thrilling aesthetic experience, and then go by public transportation to the Brooklyn Museum, our next point of focus.If you're coming from the Custom House and crossing the Brooklyn Bridge it makes a fitting passage because the Brooklyn Bridge was considered the final link in joining or uniting the furthermost eastern United States (Long Island) to the mainland and the West. Both the Custom House and the bridge speak to the ideals of Manifest Destiny and the bridge was promoted as such a link.[96]Your walk across the bridge exemplifies the linkage of Long Island to the rest of the continent.

In Brooklyn take the #2 or #3 train at Clark Street to Eastern Parkway and the Brooklyn Museum. The museum is closed Monday and Tuesday.

3. Brooklyn

Welcome To Brooklyn:
4th Largest City In America[97]

> Dere's no guy livin' that knows Brooklyn t'roo and t'roo (only the dead know Brooklyn t'roo and t'roo), because it'd take a lifetime just to find his way aroun' duh goddam town[98]

The Brooklyn Museum is the most important Piccirilli site in Brooklyn. The museum moved to its present location at 200 Eastern Parkway from the Brooklyn City Hall area and opened in 1897. (Take the 2 or 3 train to Eastern Parkway.) The land the museum is on had been intended to be used as part of Prospect Park but Frederick Law Olmstead and Calvert Vaux, (who also designed and built Central Park), did not use it for the park. The original plan for the Brooklyn Museum was by the firm of McKim, Meade and White (1897-1924). But because of budgetary restraints the building they conceived was never built. The museum was planned as a building with at least four times the size and space than the structure that exists now.[99] The museum has over 2,000,000 objects and includes an Egyptian collection rivaled only by the museums of London and Cairo. The Brooklyn Museum is ranked fifth among the museums of this country for its fine arts collection.[100]

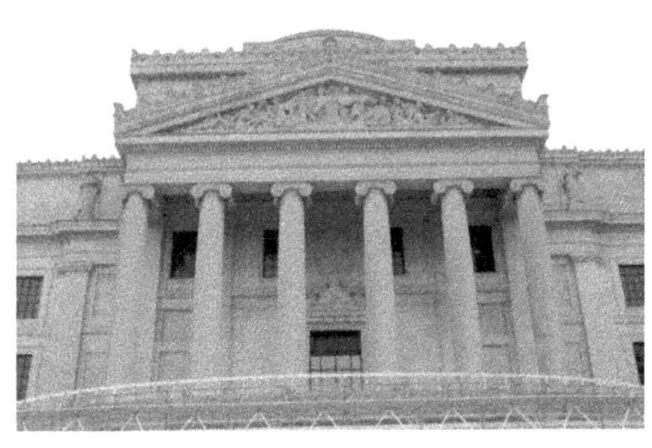

In front of the Brooklyn Museum where new construction has positioned them at the top of the new entrance steps are two large sculptures, *Brooklyn* and *Manhattan*. They are by Daniel Chester French and carved out of granite by the Piccirillis.The sculptures once graced the Brooklyn approach to the Manhattan Bridge but were removed in 1963 when the entrance to the bridge was widened. The pediment above the entrance to the museum is by Adolph Weinman and Daniel Chester French and is titled *Science and Art*. Figures representing Painting, Sculpture and Architecture are on the right and, figures representing Geology, Astronomy and Biology are on the left. A peacock is squeezed into the right corner and a sphinx is its leftmost counterpart. The peacock represents Beauty

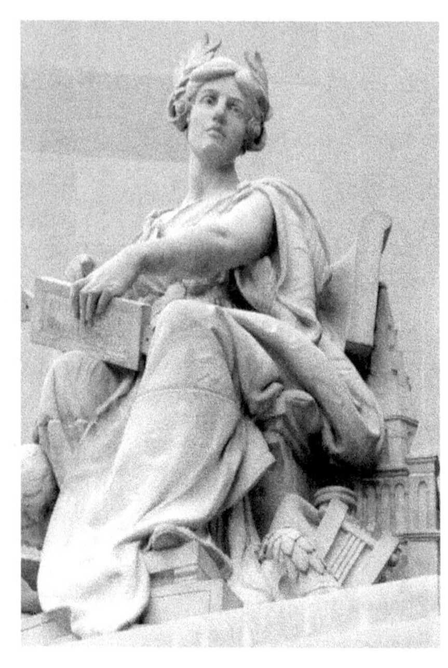

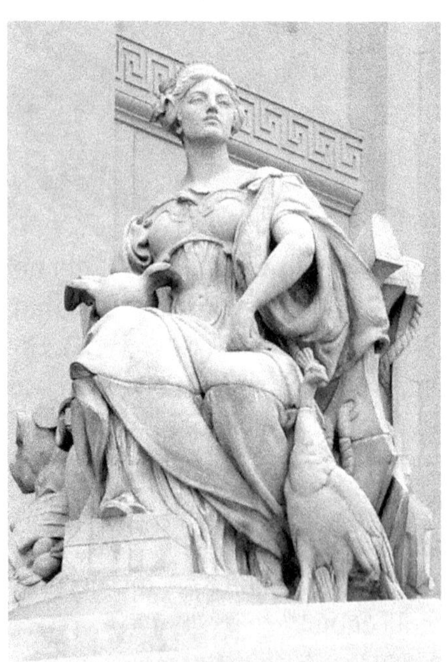

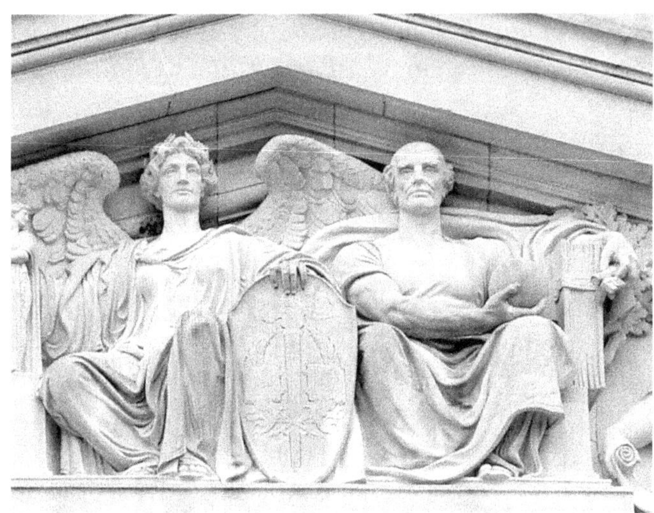

and the sphinx Knowledge. The carving was done by the Piccirillis.

Just below the roofline of the Brooklyn Museum are thirty figures representing important contributors to Western civilization. Eleven sculptors, including Attilio Piccirilli, made the sculpture. All were carved by the Piccirilli brothers. The statues, beginning with those on the Washington Avenue side of the museum are: *Zoroaster/Persian Philosophy* by Edmund T. Quinn; *Sankara/Indian Philosophy* by Edward Clark Potter; *Indian Literature/Kalidasa* and *Indian Law/Manu* by Attilio

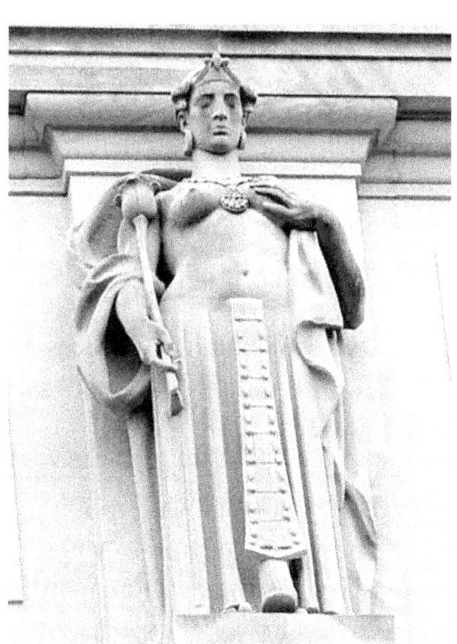

Piccirilli; *Indian Religion/Buddha* by Edward Clark Potter. At the front of museum: *Confucius/Chinese Philosophy, Lao Tse/Chinese Religion, Chinese Art* and *Chinese Law* all by Karl Bitter; *Japanese Art* by Janet Scudder; *Moses/Hebrew Law Giver, David/Hebrew Psalmist, Isaiah/Hebrew Prophet and Saint Paul/Hebrew Apostle* all by Augustus Lukeman; *Mohammed/Genius of Islam* by Charles Keck; *Homer/Greek Epic, Pindar/Greek Lyric* Poetry by Daniel Chester French; *Aeschylus/Greek Drama, Pericles/Greek State* by George T. Brewster; *Archimedes/Greek Science* by Kenyon Cox; *Minerva/Greek Religion* by Daniel Chester French; *Plato/Greek Philosophy, Phidias/Greek Architecture, Praxiteles/Greek Sculpture* and *Demosthenes/Greek Letters* all by Herbert Adams. On the west side of the museum: *Justinian/Roman Law Giver, Julius Caesar/Roman Statesman, Augustus Caesar/Roman Emperor, Cicero/Roman Orator* all by Johannes Gelert and *Virgil/Epic Poetry* by Carl Heber.[101]

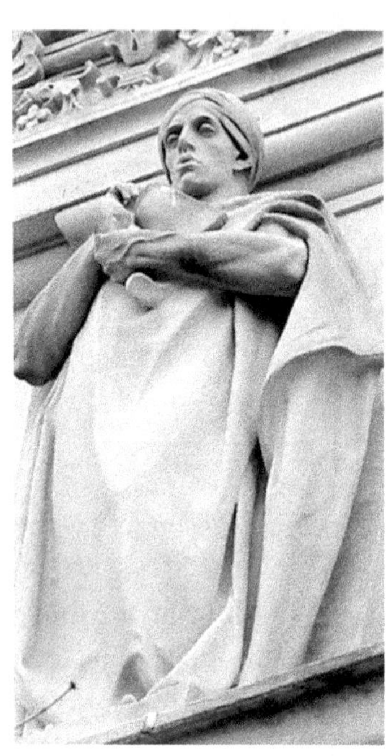

Visit the outdoor Sculpture Garden containing pieces of demolished New York City buildings and the Brooklyn Botanic Garden adjacent to the museum.

Leave the museum through the front entrance and turn left for a short walk along Eastern Parkway to Brooklyn's Grand Army Plaza and the main branch of the Brooklyn Public Library. The libraries of Brooklyn form a system separate from that of the Bronx and Manhattan. The site was chosen in 1905,

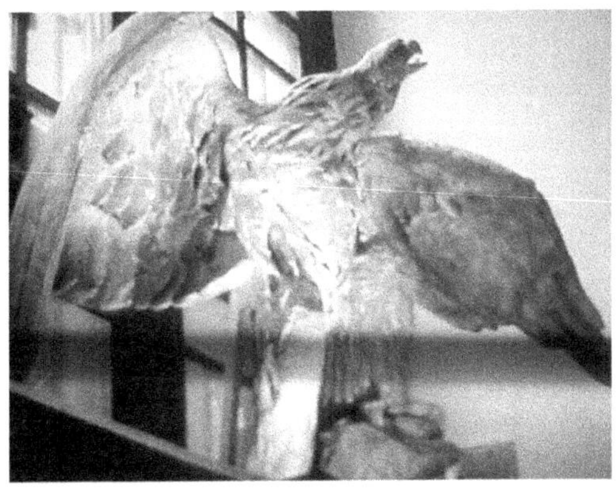

construction began in 1908, and finally was completed in 1941, a thirty-three year project. Just inside the main entrance to the library is a large cast zinc eagle made by the Piccirilli brothers for the headquarters of the *Brooklyn Eagle*.

The *Brooklyn Eagle* was a newspaper that published from 1841 to 1955. At one point in its 114 year life it was the most widely read newspaper in America. In its pages national and international news as well as local news and news of daily life in Brooklyn was published.[102]

Do not leave the area without investigating Frederick W. MacMonnies' Civil War triumphal arch honoring the soldiers and sailors who fought in the war on the Union side as well as the fountain and sculpture in the area. Take a walk in Prospect Park a park by the folks who brought you Central Park but its superior in many ways.

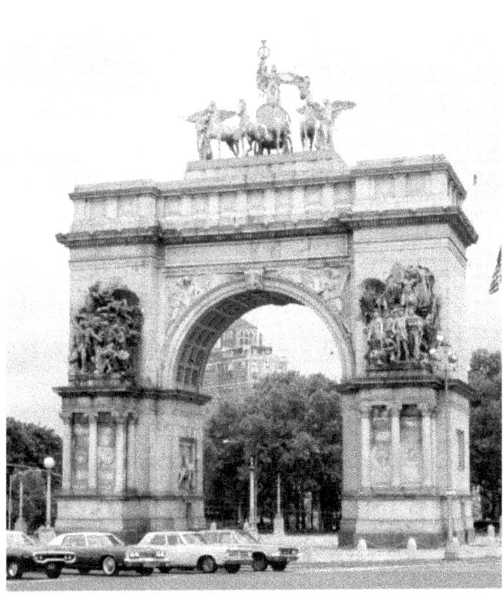

4. Queens

> Queens: a comfortable rest stop, a pleasant rung on the ladder of success, a promise we were promised in some secret dream.[103]

We leave Brooklyn for Queens, the largest borough at 115 square miles. It is also ethnically the most diverse and the last stop of this Piccirilli pilgrimage. Take the E and F train to the multi-named Union Turnpike, Queens Boulevard, Kew Gardens Station. A short walk on Queens Boulevard between Union Turnpike and 82nd Avenue will bring you to a derelict fountain surmounted by a massive statue titled *Civic Virtue* by Frederick MacMonnies. It was carved by the Piccirilli brothers and is one of the two Piccirilli works in Queens. (The other is a bust of Thomas Jefferson by Attilio Piccirilli at Queens College the bust is a bronze replica given to the college by an alumnus of the college, Mark Eisner. It is not on display.)

The monumental allegorical sculpture *Civic Virtue* is reputed to have been carved from a single block of marble, the largest carving since Michelangelo's *David.* It depicts a giant nude youth with a sword over his right shoulder who seems to be stepping on a female figure.[104] The Piccirilli brothers worked almost three years to complete the carving of this behemoth for Frederick MacMonnies. The Piccirillis neither bore any responsibility for, nor participated in the ruckus that surrounded the statue. *Civic Virtue* began its existence with its conception in 1908 and installation in City Hall Park in Manhattan fourteen years later. But, "Between the conception / And the creation / Between the emotion / And the response / Falls the Shadow"[105]

The "shadow," which includes World War I, was the more than fourteen years that had passed since MacMonnies began his work on the project and the many other important events that took place during that period. World War I may have been the most important event of the fourteen years, but the change that most affected *Civic Virtue* was the struggle of women to gain the right to vote which they had finally achieved by 1920. The politically conscious public, women in particular, were outraged to see a nude giant seemingly trampling on prostrate females and viewed the statue as anti-female. MacMonnies, who was no stranger to controversy, believed that the public was interpreting his figure too literally and attempted to explain the allegorical meaning of his figures. Allegory, shmallegory. The public was not accepting the explanation. In the past, the public whether it had understood allegorical representation or not had accepted works of art that they might not have understood. They believed that the public arts were moral and uplifting and viewed them as such. This inculcation of moral values was one of the purposes of the City Beautiful movement. After much vociferous argumentation, (with the newspapers having a field day and the mayor using the issue to enhance his standing), *Civic Virtue,* the statue, remained in City Hall Park until it was exiled to its present location in 1941 where, like John Brown's body, it lies moldering in its grave.[106]

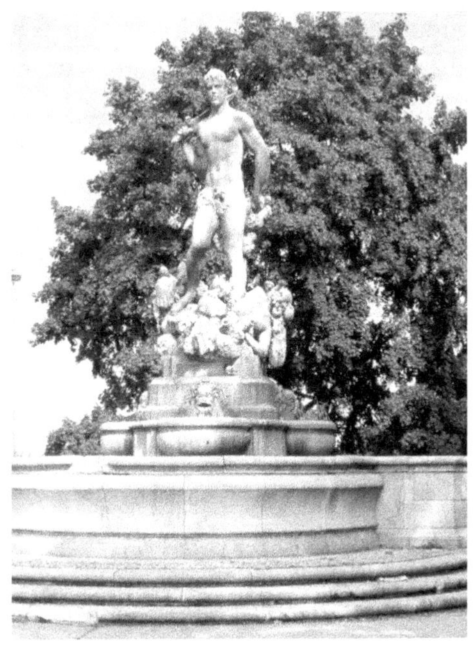

Conclusion

The end of the progressive era and the City Beautiful movement with its enhancing architecture and decorative and didactic sculpture had its demise in the 1920's. The arts and the recognizable human figure were about to face death by abstraction and the vagaries of human history and memory would consign many artists of note to anonymity. The Piccirillis are among the many.

Our revels now are over and after tip-toeing through the Piccirillis and viewing a scattering of some in New York City we may now better understand something of the extraordinary talents of the Piccirilli brothers and realize why they must be considered the foremost carvers of their time. We have seen their ability to work in any historical style from the classicism of the pediment of the New York Stock Exchange to the near abstract of the Metropolitan Museum's *Fragelina.* We have seen sculpture by the Piccirillis in a variety of styles and in a variety of materials be they carved in marble, granite, stone and wood or cast in glass, stone, zinc and bronze. Working together, the Piccirilli brothers have brought beauty to this city and freed many an angel from the stone. While their sculpture will endure, memory of them deserves a better tribute than this poor book.

Afterword

Attilio Piccirilli died October 8, 1945. His brother Getulio had died two days before on October 6, 1945.[107] Seven days after Attilio's death, on October 15, 1945 Ferruccio Piccirilli died in Poughkeepsie, N.Y. where he had been living with his son Bruno. Bruno and his wife, Maria were both teaching at Vassar College at the time. Bruno was the administrator of Attilio's estate, which had been appraised at $11,938.[108]

The Piccirilli Brothers Marble Carving Studio was sold to Gargani and Sons, bronze casters, in 1946.[109] From 1943 to April 4, 1953 the artist Alfred D. Crimi lived and worked in the studio. He occupied Attilio's room.[110] When the actual studio buildings disappeared is unknown to us.

Eleanor and Jerry Koffler

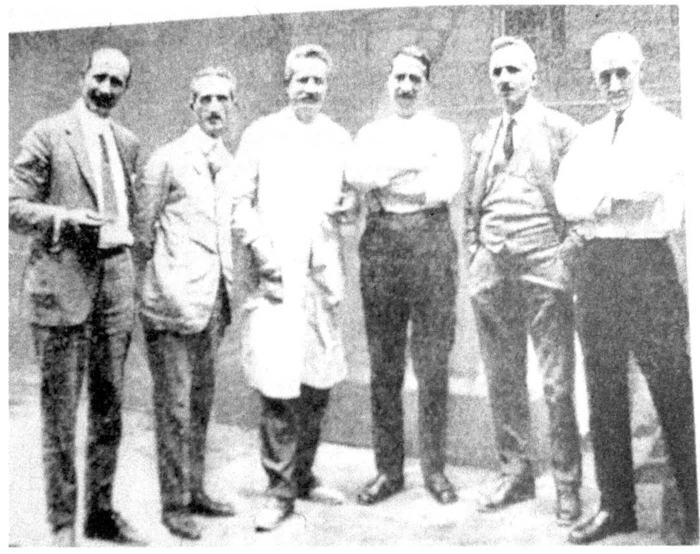

Endnotes

[1]Josef Vincent Lombardo, *Attilio Piccirilli: Life of an American Sculptor* (New York: Pitman, 1944) is almost the sole source of information about the Piccirillis. Almost anything you read about the Piccirillis, including this book, derives its information from the Lombardo book. For something of the careers of the brothers see p. 279 to 292.
[2] On March 25, 2004 East 142nd Street between Brook and Willis Avenue was changed to Piccirilli Place. Bill Carroll, another Piccirilli fan, worked assiduously with the local community board and the then City Council Member Jose M. Serrano to have the street renamed.
[3] Helen W. Henderson, *A Loiterer in New York* (New York: George H. Doran Company, 1917) p.346.
[4] Adeline Adams, "A Family of Sculptors" *The American Magazine of Art*. July,1921 Volume XII, Number 7, p.223.
[5] Thayer Tolles, ed. *American Sculpture in the Metropolitan Museum of Art: Volume I. A Catalogue of Works by Artists Born before 1865* (New York: Metropolitan Museum of Art, 1999) p.285.
[6] The recently published, *American Sculpture in the Metropolitan Museum of Art, Volume I*, edited by Thayer Tolles notes on page 233 that the sculpture was "carved by the Piccirilli Brothers and installed in the Museum in 1915." Other carvings by the Piccirilli Brothers at the Metropolitan Museum of Art but not on display that were carved for Augustus Saint-Gaudens are: a marble portrait of Homer Schiff Saint-Gaudens and both a marble relief and a bust of Louise Adele Gould. For Herbert Adams the brothers carved his *Singing Boys*. *Fragilina* and *Study of a Head* by Attilio Piccirilli and Furio's *Seal* are also in the museum collection.
[7] www.altavista.com SEARCH: Rodman Drake Poet's Corner-Joseph Rodman Drake-The Culprit Fey Page 12. Joseph Rodman Drake (1795-1820) was the son of a prominent Westchester family and is thought of as the "Poet of the Bronx." At his request he was buried in Hunts Point in the Bronx rather than in the family plot in Westchester. The first three of these lines, from a rather turgid poem, are on a plaque that is affixed to a steep rock wall along the Bronx River near the Snuff Mill in the Bronx Botanical Garden. You'll have to rappel down the cliffside or row upriver to see the plaque. Don't bother. Compare the sentiments expressed in Drake's lines with James Thurber's poem about the Bronx:

The Bronx
No thonx.

[8] The Brooklyn Museum, *The American Renaissance: 1876-1917* (New York: Pantheon Books, 1979) p.21.
[9] Bronx Home News, August 24, 1924 p.30.
[10] Lombardo, *Piccirilli,* p. 58.
[11] John McNamara, *History in Asphalt: The Origin of Bronx Street and Place Names* (Bronx, New York: The Bronx County Historical Society, 1984) p. 545.
[12] Kenneth T. Jackson ed. *The Encyclopedia of New York City* (New Havenale University Press, 1995).
Page 368 reports that the Third Avenue El was extended into the Bronx between 1886 and 1902. At one point the line, "ran on private right of way to 145th Street and followed 3rd Avenue northward." Was the private right of way made to service the Piccirilli studio also on East 142nd Street? We don't know.
[13] *Ibid.* p.144.
[14] Philip V. Cannistraro ed. *The Italians of New York: Five Centuries of Struggle and Achievement. (New York: The New York Historical Society, 1999) pp. 4-6.* For a more detailed discussion of Italian immigrationn see: Philip Cannistraro and Gerald Meyer eds., *The Lost World of Italian American Radicalism: Politics, Labor, and Culture* (West Port, Connecticut:Praeger Publishers, 2003) pp. 6-8.
[15] Lombardo, *Piccirilli*, pp. 209-215
New York Times, April 17, 1932.
[16] *Ibid.* pp. 216-217.
[17] *Ibid.* p.215.
[18] *Ibid.*, pp. 215-216.
[19] *Ibid.*, p. 216.
[20] Richman, *Daniel Chester French*, p.185 n.27.
[21] Michael T. Richman, *Daniel Chester French: An American Sculptor* (New York: Metropolitan Museum of Art, 1976), p. 23.
[22] Albert TenEyck Gardner, *American Sculpture* (New York: The Metropolitan Museum of Art, 1965) p.30.
[23] Frances Grimes quoted in, John Dryfhout, *The Work of Augustus Saint-Gaudens* (Hanover, N.H.: University Press of New England, 1982) p.31.
[24] Malvina Hoffman, *Sculpture: Inside and Out* (New York: Bonanza Books, 1939) p.158.
[25] Lombardo, *Piccirilli,* p. 245. For a fuller account of the process see pages 243-248.
[26] Wayne Craven, *Sculpture In America* (Newark: University of Delaware Press, 1984) pp. 106-107.
[27] Nathaniel Hawthorne, *The Marble Faun* (New York: Signet Classic, 1961) pp.88-89.

[28] Albert TenEyck Gardner, *American Sculpture: A Catalogue of the Collection of the Metropolitan Museum of Art* (New York: The Metropolitan Museum of Art, 1965) p.94.

[29] *The Bronx County Historical Society Journal*. Fall, 1974 pp.51-70.

[30]Beside the previously mentioned *Lincoln Memorial* and *Dupont Circle Fountain* memorials to Marconi, General Meade, Columbus, the Titanic and the First Division and about 50 other works were done by the Piccirillis in Washington, D.C.

[31] Quoted in, Douglas Keister, *Going Out In Style: The Architecture of Eternity* (New York: Facts On File, Inc., 1997), p.20.

[32] Keister, *Going Out In Style*, pp. 14-20.

[33] Edward Streeter, *The Story of The Woodlawn Cemetery* (New York: The Woodlawn Cemetery, nd), pp. 18-19.

[34] Edward F. Bergman. Woodlawn *Remembers: Cemetery of American History* (Utica, New York: North Country Books, Inc.) p. 28.

[35] Donald Martin Reynolds, *Monuments and Masterpieces* (New York:MacMillan Publishing Company, 1988) pp. 351-352.

[36] *Daily News*, February 12, 1985.

[37] Lombardo, *Piccirilli*, p. 168

[38] Conversation with Susan Olsen director of The Friends of Woodlawn Cemetery on May 18, 2003.

[39] For a fuller presentation of LaGuardia's early life see: Arthur Mann, *LaGuardia: A fighter Against His Times 1882-1933* (New York: J.B. Lippincott Company, 1959) pages 19-42 or *Thomas Kessner. Fiorello H. LaGuardia and the Making of Modern New York* (New York: McGraw-Hill Publishing Company,1989) pages 3-26.

[40] Mann. p.62

[41] See map listing: *Woodlawn's Famous* "Political Hall of Fame." At E-4 is the number "6" in light numbers. The grave abuts Alpine Avenue.

[42] Lombardo, *Piccirilli*, p.197.

[43] Mann, p.138.

[44] Kessner, *LaGuardia*, p 82.

[45] Mann, *LaGuardia*, p.250.

[46] Mann, *LaGuardia*, p.250.

[47] Cesar Andreu Iglesias ed. *Memoirs of Bernardo Vega* (New York: Monthly Review Press, 1984) p.6.

[48] Iglesias, *Bernardo Vega*, p.11.

[49] James M. Dennis. *Karl Bitter: Architectural Sculptor 1867-1915* (Madison: The University of Wisconsin Press, 1967) pp.3-36.

[50] Helen W. Henderson, *A Loiterer in New York* (New York: George H. Doran Company, 1917) p. 376.

[51] Dennis, Karl Bitter, p.283, note 6.

[52] Robert A.M. Stern, *New York 1930:Architecture and Urbanism Between the Two World Wars* (New York: Rizzoli, 1987) p.154 The wealthy of the Gilded Age (1865-1920) were conscious of their obligation to use some of their fortunes to help others less fortunate. To promote and establish a wide range of charitable activities John D. Rockefeller Sr. had a clergyman, Rev. Frederick Gates, assist him in doling out his money. For a similar feeling of obligation John D. Jr. built Riverside Church to give the views of Dr. Harry Emerson Fosdick wider dissemination.
[53] From a 1930 Hearst newspaper series. The newspaper and its date are not known.
[54] Beatrice Gilman Proske. *Brookgreen Gardens Sculpture.* (Brookgreen Gardens. , S.C., 1968) p.439.
[55] *Ibid.* p.102. Also see: Lombardo, *Piccirilli* p.282-291.
[56] From an unpublished manuscript, courtesy of Victor Jordan archivist at The Riverside Church Archives.
[57] *New York Times*, April 10, 1910, page.7.
[58] Henderson, *A Loiterer in New York.* p.359.
[59] *New York Times* of February 15, 1908 page 3. A second article describes the ceremonies attendant to the unveiling of the *Firemen's Memorial* that was made to honor fire fighters who died in the line of duty. The death of Deputy Chief Kruger was its inspiration. See: *New York Times* for September 6, 1913, page 4.
[60] An excellent account of the *grosse geschichte* can be found in, Michelle H. Bogart, *Public Sculpture and the Civic Ideal in New York City:1890-1930* (Washington: Smithsonian Institution Press, 1977) pages 185-217. An earlier version of the same subject by the same author, "Maine Monument and Pulitzer Fountain—A Study in Patronage and Process" can be found on pages 41-63 of *Winterhur Portfolio* 21, no. 1 (Spring, 1986).
[61] *London Evening Mail*, December 5, 1912.
[62] Lombardo, *Piccirilli*, p.129. The Hearst Collection has no record of it ever being in its collection.
[63] Reynolds, *Monuments and Masterpieces*, p.352.
[64] *London Evening Mail*, December 5, 1912.
[65] Bogart, *Public Sculpture*, p.197.
[66] *Ibid,* pp. 109-202.
[67] Paul Goldberger, *The City Observed: New York* (New York: Vintage Books, 1979) p.181. A new plan for traffic circulation was proposed and construction is underway at this writing (May, 2004).
[68] From the information placard at the Metropolitan Museum of Art for *The Children of Prescott Hall Butler,* marble relief.
[69] Richmond, *French*, pp.71-79.

[70] Craven, *Sculpture in America* p.235.
[71] *Ibid.*, p.402.
[72] The information about the Homestead Strike was culled from the program transcript for, *The American Experience: Andrew Carnegie.*The internet address is: www.pbs.org/.
[73] Beatrice Gilman Proske, *Brookgreen Gardens Sculpture* (Brookgreen Gardens, S.C., 1968) p.102.
[74] Margot Gayle and Michele Cohen, *The Art Commission and the Municipal Art Society Guide to Manhattan's Outdoor Sculpture* (New York:Prentice Hall Press, 1988) pp.192-193.
[75] Elliot Willensky and Norval White, *AIA Guide to New York City* 3rd ed. (New York: Harcourt Brace Jovanovich Publishers, 1988) p.272.
[76] Joseph Lederer, *All Around the Town* (New York: Charles Scribner's Sons: 1975) p.100-101.
[77] Christine Roussel, *The Art of Rockefeller Center.* (New York: W. W. Norton & Company, 2006)
[78] Christine Smith, *St. Bartholomew's Church in the City of New York* (New York: Oxford University Press, 1988) p.16.
[79] Percy Preston Jr., *Saint Bartholomew's Church in the City of New York: An Architectural Tour* (New York: Saint Bartholomew's Church, 1998), pp.16-17.
[80] Donald Martin Reynolds, *Monuments and Masterpieces* (New York: Macmillan Publishing Company, 1988) p. 262.
[81] Smith, *St. Bartholomew's*, p. 128.
[82] Carol von Pressentin Wright, *Blue Guide: New York* (New York: W.W. Norton & Company Inc, 1991) p.323.
[83] Henry Hope Reed, *The New York Public Library* (New York: W.W. Norton & Company, 1986) p.48.
[84] Henderson, *A Loiterer in New York*, p.204.
[85] *Ibid.* p.206.
[86] *Ibid.* pp.181-182. In *The Island at the Center of the World: The Epic Story of Dutch Manhattan and the Forgotten Colony That Shaped America* by Russel Shorto (Doubleday: New York, 2004) page 233. It is suggested that Greenwich Village might have received its name from, "a settler from the Long Island village Greenwyck (Pine District) [who] would relocate here and give his property that name."
[87] See pages 233-234 of *The Island at the Center of the World.* The book is cited in note 85 above.
[88] Dore Ashton, *Noguchi East and West* (Berkeley: University of California Press, 1992) pages 13 and 299.
[89] *The Bronx Home News,* August 24, 1924, p.30.

[90] The medal is on display at the Police Museum at 100 Old Slip south of the South Street Seaport.
[91] Albert TenEyck Gardner, *American Sculpture*, (New York: The Metropolitan Museum of Art, 1965) p.31.
[92] From the *North Side News,* 1923. No other date or page information available. The newspaper article is on file at the Bronx Historical Society.
[93] Bogart, *Public Sculpture*, p.121.
[94] The Gilded Age, an era of American history from after the Civil War to about World War I, continued the doctrine of Manifest Destiny. The following quotation is from a speech by Senator Albert Beveridge in 1900 and may be found in the *Congressional Record*, 56th Cong. 1st Sess.., 704-712. "…Mr. President, this question is deeper than any question of party politics; deeper than any question of the isolated policy of our country; deeper even than any question of constitutional policy. It is elemental. It is racial. God has not been preparing the English-speaking and Teutonic peoples for a thousand years for nothing but vain and idle self-contemplation and self-admiration. No! He has made us the master organizers of the world to establish system where chaos reigns. He has given us the spirit of progress to overwhelm the forces of reaction throughout the earth. He has made us adept in government that we may administer government among savage and senile peoples. Were it not for such force as this the world would relapse into barbarism and night. And of all our race He has marked the American people as His chosen nation to finally lead in the regeneration of the world. This is the divine mission of America, and it holds for us all the profit, all the glory, all the happiness possible to man. We are trustees of the world's progress, guardians of the righteous peace. The judgment of the Master is upon us: 'Ye have been faithful over a few things; I will make you ruler over many things.'"
[95] Bogart, *Public Sculpture*, pages 130-134.
[96] Brooklyn Museum, *The Great East River Bridge: 1883-1983* (New York: Harry N. Abrams, Inc., 1983) pp.10-11.
[97] Rita Seiden Miller ed., *Brooklyn USA: The Fourth Largest City in America* (New York: Brooklyn College Press, 1979) p.3.
[98] From "Only the Dead Know Brooklyn" by Francis E. Skipp ed., *The Complete Short Stories of Thomas Wolfe*. (New York: Scribner, 1987) p.260.
[99] Carol Lopate, *Education and Culture in Brooklyn: A History of Ten Institutions* (Brooklyn, N.Y.: The Brooklyn Educational and Cultural Alliance, 1979) Pamphlet, pages 35-39.
[100] Nanette Rainone ed., *The Brooklyn Neighborhood Book* (Brooklyn, N.Y.: The Fund for the Borough of Brooklyn, Inc, 1985) Pamphlet, page 62.

[101] Bogart, *Public Sculpture,* pages 165-176.
[102] From: *Brooklyn Daily Eagle On Line: 1841-1902* on the internet.
[103] John Guare, Introduction to *The House of Blue Leaves*
[104] Federal Writers Project, *New York City Guide* (New York: Octagon Books, 1970) p.97.
[105] Thomas Stearns Eliot. *The Complete Poems and Plays: 1909-1950.* pp.56-59, stanza V.
[106] For a comprehensive discussion of the trials and tribulations of *Civic Virtue* see the previously cited *Public Sculpture and the Civic Ideal in New York* by Michele Bogart, pages 259-270.
[107] *New York Herald*, October 9, 1945.
[108] *Poughkeepsie New Yorker*, June 21, 1950.
[109] *Bronx Home News*, August 27, 1946. p.17.
[110] Alfred E. Crimi. *A Look Back A Step Foward: My Life Story.*(Staten Island, N.Y.: Center for Migration Studies, 1987) p. 167.

Selected Bibliography

Adams, Adeline. "A Family of Sculptors" *The American Magazine of Art*. (July,1921), Volume XII, Number 7, p.223.

Allen, James. *Without Sanctuary*. Santa Fe: Twin Palms Publishers, 2000.

Applebaum, Stanley. *The Chicago World's Fair of 1893: A Photographic Record.* New York: Dover Publications Inc., 1980.

Applebaum, Stanley. *The New York World's Fair 1939/1940.* New York: Dover Publications, 1977.

Ashton, Dore. *Noguchi East and West.* Berkeley: University of California Press, 1992

Bogart, Michele H. *Maine Monument and Pulitzer Fountain, A Study in Patronage and Progress.* Winterthur Portfolio 21, No. 1, Spring, 1986, pp.41-63.

——— *Public Sculpture and the Civic Ideal in New York City, 1890-1930.* Washington: Smithsonian Institution Press, 1977.

Bridges, William. *Gathering of Animals, An Unconventional History of the New York Zoological Society.* New York: Harper and Row, Publishers, 1974.

Bronx County Historical Society Journal. Fall, 1974.

Bronx Home News. August 24, 1924, p.30.

Bronx Home News. August 27, 1940. p.17.

Brooklyn Museum. *The American Renaissance: 1876-1917.* New York: Pantheon Books, 1979.

Bzdak, Meredith Ames. *Public Sculpture in New Jersey: Monuments to a Collective Identity.* New Brunswick, N.J.: Rutgers University Press, 1999.

Cannistraro, Philip V. ed. *The Italians of New York: Five Centuries of Struggle and Achievement.* New York: The New York Historical Society, 1999.

Capa, Jerry. *A Friendship with Attilio Piccirilli.* Booklet, privately published, 1999.

Conner - Rosenkranz. *Rediscoveries in American Sculpture: Studio Works, 1893-1939.* Austin: The University of Texas Press, 1989.

——— *American Sculpture, 1845-1925*. New York: Conner - Rosencranz, 1999.

——— *American Sculpture, 1845-1925.* New York: Conner - Rosencranz, 2001.

——— *American Sculpture 1850-1950.* New York: Conner - Rosencranz, 2003.

Crane, Sylvia E. *White Silence: Greenough, Powers, and Crawford American Sculptors in Nineteenth-Century Italy.* Coral Gables: University of Miami Press, 1972.
Craven, Wayne. *Sculpture In America.* Newark: University of Delaware Press, 1984.
Crimi, Alfred D. *A Look Back, a Look Forward: My Life Story*. Staten Island: Center for Migration Studies, 1987.
Culbertson, Judi and Tom Randall. *Permanent New Yorkers.* Chelsea, Vermont: Chelsea Green Publishing Company, 1987.
Daily News, February 12, 1985.
Dennis, James M. *Karl Bitter: Architectural Sculptor 1867-1915.* Madison: The University of Wisconsin Press, 1967.
Dolkart, Andrew S. *Morningside Heights: A History of the Architecture and Development.* New York: Columbia University Press, 1998.
Dryfhout, John. *The Work of Augustus Saint-Gaudens.* Hanover, N.H: University Press of New England, 1982.
Duby, George and Jean-Luc Daval eds., *Sculpture from Antiquity to Present Day,* New York: Taschen, 2002.
Dunlap, David W. *On Broadway, A Journey Uptown Over Time.* New York: Rizzoli International Press, 1990.
Eliot, T. S. *The Complete Poems and Plays: 1909-1950.* New York: Harcourt, Brace and Company, 1952.
Evert, Marilyn. *Discovering Pittsburgh's Sculpture*. Pittsburgh, Pa.: The University of Pittsburgh Press, 1983.
Fairman, Charles E. *Art and Artists of the Capitol of the United States of America.* Washington: United States Government Printing Office, 1927.
Federal Writers Project. *New York City Guide.* New York: Octagon Books, 1970.
Francisco, Charles. *Radio City Music Hall, An Affectionate History of the World's Greatest Theater.* New York: E. P. Dutton, 1979.
Fried, Frederick and Edmund V. Gillon, Jr., *New York Civic Sculpture: A Pictorial Guide.* NewYork: Dover Publications, Inc., 1976.
Gambino, Richard. *Blood of My Blood.* New York: Anchor Books, 1974.
Gardner, Albert Ten Eyck. *American Sculpture: A Catalogue of the Collection of the Metropolitan Museum of Art.* New York: The Metropolitan Museum of Art, 1965.
Gayle, Margot and Michelle Cohen. *Manhattan's Outdoor Sculpture.* New York: Prentice Hall Press, 1988.
Gerdts, William H. *American Neo-Classic Sculpture The Marble Resurrection.* New York: The Viking Press, 1973.

Goldberger, Paul. *The City Observed: New York.* New York: Vintage Books, 1979.

Goode, James M. *The Outdoor Sculpture of Washington D. C.: A Comprehensive Historical Guide.* Washington, D. C.: Smithsonian Institution Press, 1974.

Greenthal, Kathryn, Paula M. Kozol, Jan Seidler Ramirez, *American Figurative Sculpture in the Museum of Fine Arts Boston.* Boston: Museum of Fine Arts, 1986.

Groce, Nancy, *New York: Songs of the City*. New York: Watson Guptill Publications, 1999.

Gurney, George. *Sculpture and The Federal Triangle.* Washington, D. C.: Smithsonian Institution Press, 1985.

Hawthorne, Nathaniel. *The Marble Faun*. New York: The New American Library, Inc., 1961.

Henderson, Helen W. *A Loiterer in New York.* New York: George H. Doran Company, 1917.

Hoffman, Malvina. *Sculpture: Inside and Out.* New York: Bonanza Books, 1939.

Howard, Shirley Reiff. *C. Paul Jennewein.* Tampa, Florida: The Tampa Museum, 1980.

Iglesias, Cesar Andreu, ed. *Memoirs of Bernardo Vega.* New York: Monthly Review Press, 1984.

Irish, Sharon, *Cass Gilbert: Architect: Modern Traditionalist*. New York: Monacelli Press, 1999.

Jackson, Kenneth T. ed. *The Encyclopedia of New York City.* New Haven: Yale University Press, 1995.

Jacoby, Stephen M.. *Architectural Sculpture in New York City.* New York: Dover Publication, Inc., 1975.

Jaffe, Irma ed., *The Italian Presence in American Arts 1760-1860.* New York, Fordham University Press, 1989.

——— *The Italian Presence in American Art, 1860-1920*. New York, Fordham University Press, 1992.

Joint Committee on the Library. *Art in the United States Capitol.* Washington: United States Government Printing Office, 1978.

Keister, Douglas. *Going Out In Style: The Architecture of Eternity.* New York: Facts On File, Inc., 1997.

Kessner, Thomas. *Fiorello H. LaGuardia and the Making of Modern New York*. New York: McGraw Hill Publishing Company, 1989.

Krinsky, Carol Herselle. *Rockefeller Center.* New York: Oxford University Press, 1978.

Landau, Sarah Bradford. *George B. Post, Architect: Picturesque Designer and Determined Realist.* New York: The Monacelli Press, Inc., 1998.

Lederer, Joseph. *All Around the Town.* New York: Charles Scribner's Sons.1975.

Lombardo, Josef Vincent. *Attilio Piccirilli: Life of an American Sculptor.* New York: Pitman, 1944.

Lopate, Carol. *Education and Culture in Brooklyn: A History of Ten Institutions.* Brooklyn, N.Y.: The Brooklyn Educational and Cultural Alliance, 1979.

Mangione, Jerre and Ben Morreale. *La Storia.* New York: HarperCollins Publishers, 1993.

Mann, Arthur. *LaGuardia: A Fighter Against His Times 1882-1933.* New York: J.B. Lippincott Company, 1959.

McNamara, John. *History in Asphalt: The Origin of Bronx Street and Place Names.* Bronx, New York:The Bronx County Historical Society, 1984.

Miller, Rita Seiden, ed. *Brooklyn USA: The Fourth Largest City in America.* New York: Brooklyn College Press, 1979.

Modern Sculpture: Scrapbook of Reproductions. New York Public Library, 1939.

Nuehaus, Eugen, *The Art of the Exposition: Personal Impressions of the Architecture, Sculpture, Mural Decorations , Color Scheme and Other Aethestic Aspects of the Panama-Pacific International Exposition.* San Francisco: Paul Elder and Company, 1915.

New York Times. February 15, 1908, p.3.

New York Times. April 10, 1910, p.7.

New York Times. September 6, 1913, p.4.

Orsi, Robert Anthony. *The Madonna of 115th Street.* New Haven: Yale University Press, 1985.

Preston, Percy Jr. *Saint Bartholomew's Church in the City of New York: An Architectural Tour.* New York: Saint Bartholomew's Church, 1998.

Proske, Beatrice Gilman. *Brookgreen Gardens Sculpture.* Brookgreen Gardens, S.C., 1968.

Quirk, Howard E. *The Living Cathedral of St. John the Devine: A History and Guide.* New York:The Crossroad Publishing Company, 1993.

Rainone, Nanette, ed. *The Brooklyn Neighborhood Book.* Brooklyn, N.Y.: The Fund for the Borough of Brooklyn, Inc. 1985.

Rand, Harry. *Paul Manship.* Washington, D. C.: National Museum of American Art, Smithsonian Institution Press, 1989.

Reed, Henry Hope. *The New York Public Library.* New York: W.W. Norton & Company, 1986.

Reynolds, Donald Martin. *The Architecture of New York City.* New York: Macmillam Publishing Company, 1984.

——— *Monuments and Masterpiece.* New York: MacMillan Publishing Company, 1988.

Rosenfield, Lucy D.A., *A Century of American Sculpture: The Roman Bronze Works Foundry.* Atglen, Pa: Schiffer Publishing Ltd., 2002.

Roussel, Christine. *The Art of Rockefeller Center.* New York: W. W. Norton & Company, 2006.

———*The Guide to the Art of Rockefeller Center.* New York: W. W. Norton & Company, 2006.

Richman, Michael T. *Daniel Chester French: An American Sculptor.* New York: Metropolitan Museum of Art, 1976.

Riverside Church. *Architecture and Symbolism of the Riverside Church.* New York: Riverside Church 1930.

Rozas, Diane. *American Venus, The Extraordinary Life of Audrey Munson Model and Muse.* Los Angeles: Balcony Press, 1999.

Senie, Harriet F. and Sally Webster eds. *Crtical Issues in Public Art, Content, Context and Controversy.* Washington D. C.: Smithsonian Institution Press, 1998.

Sharp, Lewis I. *John Quincy Adams Ward: Dean of American Sculpture.* Newark: University of Delaware Press, 1985.

——— *New York City Public Sculpture by 19th Century American Artists.* New York: The Metropolitan Museum of Art, 1974.

Shelley, Mary and Bill Carroll. "Carving America'a Monuments: The Piccirilli brothers of the Bronx." *Bronx Times.* July 15, 1999 pp.6-7.

——— "The Piccirilli Brothers: Carvers of History" *Ambassador: National Italian American Quarterly.* (Winter, 2002) no. 50, pp.2-9.

——— "The Piccirilli Studio" *The Bronx County Historical Journal* (Spring, 1999) vol. XXXVI no.1 pp. 1-12.

Shorto, Russell, *The Island at the Center of the World: The Epic Story of Dutch Manhattan and the Forgotten Colony that Shaped America,* New York: Doubleday, 2004.

Siris. Smithsonian Inventory of American Sculpture. [Internet Address: www.siris.si.edu]

Smith, Christine. *St. Bartholomew's Church in the City of New York.* New York: Oxford University Press, 1988.

Soria, Regina, *American Artists of Italian Heritage 1776-1945: A Bibliographical Dictionary,* Cranbury, NJ, Associated University Presses, 1993.

Stern, Robert A.M., Gregory Gilmartin and John Massengale. *Metropolitan Architecture and Urbanism 1890- 1915.* New York: Rizzoli International Publications, 1995.

Streeter, Edward. *The Story of The Woodlawn Cemetery.* New York: The Woodlawn Cemetery, nd.

Taft, Lorado. *The History of American Sculpture.* New York: The Macmillan Company, 1903.

The National Sculpture Society. *Contemporary American Sculpture.* New York: Press of the Kalkhoff Company, 1929.

Tolles, Thayer ed. *American Sculpture in the Metropolitan Museum of Art: Volume I. A Catalogue of Works by Artists Born before 1865.* New York: The Metropolitan Museum of Art, 1999.

———— *American Sculpture in the Metropolitan Museum of Art: Volume II. A Catalogue of Works by Artists Born between 1865 and 1885.* New York: The Metropolitan Museum of Art, 2001.

———— *Perspectives on American Sculpture.* New York: The Metropolitan Museum of Art, 2003.

Vass, Frederick S. *John Frazee, Sculptor.* Washington City: National Portrait Gallery, Smithsonian Institution, 1986.

Voorsanger, Catherine Hoover and John Howat. eds. *Art and the Empire City: New York, 1825-1861.* New York: The Metropolitan Museum of Art. 2000.

Wilkinson, Burke. *The Life and Works of Augustus Saint Gaudens.* New York: Dover Publications Inc., 1985.

Willensky, Elliot and Norval White. *AIA Guide to New York City* 3rd ed.. New York: Harcourt Brace, Jovanovich Publishers, 1988.

Winwar, Frances. *Ruotolo, Man and Artist.* New York: Liveright Publishing Corporation, 1949.

Whitney Museum. *200 years of American Sculpture.* New York: Whitney Museum of American Art 1971.

Wolff, Wendy ed. *Capitol Builders: The Shorthand Journals of Montgomery C. Meigs, 1853-1859*, 1861. Washington, D.C.: U.S. Government Printing Office, 2001.

Index

Comprehensive Listing of Piccirilli Sculpture by Borough

List of Abbreviations

BCHS	Bronx County Historical Society
Ch	Church
CU	Columbia University
G	Gallery
Miseri	Misericordia
MCNY	Museum of the City of New York
MMA	Metropolitan Museum of Art
MS	Middle School
NYPL	New York Public Library
NYSE	New York Stock Exchange
PBMCS	Piccirilli Brothers Marble Carving Studio
RC	Rockefeller Center
St. Bart’s	St. Bartholomew’s Church
tymp	tympanum

1. Piccirilli sculpture in the Bronx

The first column has the name of the sculptor. The second column has the carver's name. A blank space in the second column indicates that we assume the sculptor carved the piece. The third column has the name of the sculpture and the fourth its general location.

SCULPTOR	CARVER	TITLE	LOCATION
Piccirilli, Attilio		Leonardo Da Vinci	M.S. 45 Bronx
Piccirilli, Attilio		Christopher Columbus	Park at Crescent and Arthur Avenues.
Piccirilli, Attilio		Mother (Josephine L. Newcomb)	BCHS
Piccirilli, Attilio		The Outcast	Woodlawn Cemetery
Piccirilli, Attilio		Mother and Child	Woodlawn Cemetery
Piccirilli, Attilio		LaGuardia Grave Memorial	Woodlawn Cemetery
Piccirilli, Attilio	PBMCS	Mother and Child (De Blasio)	Woodlawn Cemetery
Piccirilli, Attilio	PBMCS	Edwin Blashfield Memorial	Woodlawn Cemetery
Aitken , Robert	PBMCS	Bliss Memorial	Woodlawn Cemetery
French, D.C.	PBMCS	Kinsley Memorial	Woodlawn Cemetery
Korbel, Mario J.	PBMCS	Joseph Stransky Memorial	Woodlawn Cemetery
Furio Piccirilli		The Ostrich	Private Collection

A note about the Manhattan entries

Every attempt has been made to present an accurate list of the sculpture carved by the Piccirillis. But the paucity of specific information, especially about their role in carving the numerous architectural and decorative sculptures for Riverside Church and St. Bartholomew's Churches in Manhattan, makes for a degree of speculation that qualifies as an "educated guess."

The amount of stone carving that the Piccirillis did for Riverside Church and St. Bartholomew's Church is mind-boggling. The publications from the churches that we used, part of our cache of source material provided by the archivists, Mr. Victor Jordan of Riverside Church and Mr. Percy Preston Jr. of Saint Bartholomew's Church, attempt to be as informative as possible as the books undertake to describe all that is interesting in their respective churches. Stained glass windows, tile mosaics, iron work, wood carvings, bronze work, church organs, paintings, architectural features and stone carvings are but some of the wealth of detail that are described in the church publications. While these publications have been extremely useful and comprehensive, the sheer volume of subject matter precludes having the finite detail we would so much love to have. Unfortunately, until research beyond the scope of this small book is done, the ambiguity of an educated guess must stand for some of the entries for these two churches.

We have omitted for future research and clarification listing the sculpture believed to be carved by Bruno Piccirilli for the Cathedral of Saint John the Divine and St. Patrick's Cathedral. We know for a certainty from the materials provided by the archivist at St. John the Divine that Bruno was an assistant to John Angel (1881-1960) the sculptor of record for the North Tower Porch, the Central Porch and the South Tower Porch as well as other sculpture for the church. What is not known with exactitude are the years when Bruno worked as Angel's assistant. We have evidence that Bruno worked for John Angel from 1951 to 1960, the year of Angel's death. What is unclear is whether Bruno began working for Angel in 1947. The son of John Angel wrote that his father worked at the Cathedral between 1925 and 1940. This is in conflict with the above and with other information we have.

John Angel also did work for St. Patrick's Cathedral. Information about Bruno having sculpture in St. Patrick's Cathedral is inconclusive so we made no listing for St. Patrick's. A project we were unable to pursue and leave for future research is that of research at Temple Emanu-El. We suspect that there is a Piccirilli connection to the carvings at Temple Emanu-El.

2. Piccirilli sculpture in Manhattan

The first column has the name of the sculptor. The second column has the carvers name. A blank space in the second column indicates that we assume the sculptor carved the piece. The third column has the name of the sculpture and the fourth its general location.

The last seventeen entries for Riverside Church will have in the third column a number. This number denotes the number of individual figures that make up the full sculpture. Detailed information about these seventeen entries is not available. The number is our count or estimate.

SCULPTOR	CARVER	TITLE	LOCATION
Piccirilli, Attilio		Nude with Broken Pitcher	Natl. Acad. Design
Piccirilli, Attilio		Firemen's Memorial	Riverside Dr.+W.100
Piccirilli, Attilio		Fragelina, bronze	Unknown
Piccirilli, Attilio		Fragelina, marble	Unknown
Piccirilli, Attilio		Fragelina	LaGuardia Newsreel
Piccirilli, Attilio		Maine Monument	Columbus Circle
Piccirilli, Attilio	PBMCS	Christopher Columbus	Columbus Citizen Foundation @ 69th St.
Piccirilli, Attilio		Courage, Study in plaster	City Hall Art Comm.
Piccirilli, Attilio	PBMCS	Atlantic	MCNY
Piccirilli, Attilio		Joy of Life	RC 15 West 48th St.

Piccirilli, Attilio		Wisdom, Sound & Light	RC above 49th St. entrance
Piccirilli, Attilio		Youth Leading Industry	RC 636 5th Ave.
Piccirilli, Attilio	PBMCS	Commerce and Industry	RC 636 5th Ave.
Lentelli, Leo	PBMCS	Four Continents	RC 636 5th Ave.
Lentelli, Leo	PBMCS	Four Periods in Italian History	RC 7th Floor spandrels Palazzo D'Italia
Janniot, Alfred	PBMCS	Gallic Freedom	RC 610 5th Ave.
Jennewein, Carl Paul	PBMCS	Coat of Arms Great Britain	RC 620 5th Ave.
Lawrie, Lee	PBMCS	The Story of Mankind	RC 29 West 50th St.
Lawrie, Lee	PBMCS	World Peace	RC 29 West 50th St.
Lawrie, Lee	PBMCS	Progress	RC above 49th St. entrance
Piccirilli, Attilio		Study of a Head	MMA
Piccirilli, Attilio		Fragelina	MMA
Piccirilli, Furio		Seal	MMA
Burroughs, Edith W.	PBMCS	At the Threshold	MMA
French, D.C.	PBMCS	The Milmore Memorial	MMA
French, D.C.	PBMCS	Mourning Victory	MMA
French, D.C.	PBMCS	Memory	MMA
Bartlett, Paul W.	PBMCS	Clinton Oglive	MMA
Bartlett, Paul W.	PBMCS	Philosophy	NYPL
Bartlett, Paul W.	PBMCS	Romance	NYPL
Bartlett, Paul W.	PBMCS	Religion	NYPL
Bartlett, Paul W.	PBMCS	Poetry	NYPL
Bartlett, Paul W.	PBMCS	Drama	NYPL

Bartlett, Paul W.	PBMCS	History	NYPL
Potter, Edward C.	PBMCS	Library Lions	NYPL
Calder, Alexander S.	PBMCS	G. Washington as President	Wash. Sq. Arch
MacMonnies, Fred.	PBMCS	Spandrel Panel	Wash. Sq. Arch
MacNeil, Hermon A	PBMCS	Washington as Comm. Chief	Wash. Sq. Arch
Piccirilli, Furio		Penguin	Natl. Acad.Design
Ward, J.Q.A.	Getulio Piccirilli	Pediment	NYSE
Corrado, Novany	PBMCS	Waldo Hutchins Bench	5th Ave. @ 72nd St. Central Park
Bitter, Karl	PBMCS	Pulitzer Fountain	Fifth + 58
Piccirilli, Orazio		Horns of Plenty	Fifth + 58
French, D.C.	PBMC S	Africa	Custom House
French, D.C.	PBMC S	America	Custom House
French, D.C.	PBMCS	Asia	Custom House
French, D.C.	PBMCS	Europe	Custom House
Piccirilli, Attilio		Orpheus, pediment	Frick Museum
Piccirilli, Attilio		Sculpture, pediment	Frick Museum
Piccirilli, Attilio		Policemen's Memorial Mon.	Police Headquarters
Piccirilli, Attilio		Young Faun	Private Collection Courtesy of Conner Rosenkranz, NY
Piccirilli, Attilio		Young Virgin	Private Collection Courtesy of Conner Rosenkranz, NY

Piccirilli, Attilio		Head of a Boy	Private Collection, NY
Piccirilli, Attilio		Head of a Woman	Private Collection, NY
Piccirilli, Attilio		Atlantic Sketch for Maine Monument	Private Collection, NY
PBMCS	PBMCS	Fireplace Surround	Private Collection, NY
Piccirilli, Attilio		Head of A Boy	Conner Rosenkranz, NY
Piccirilli, Attilio		Head of a Woman	Conner Rosenkranz, NY
Piccirilli, Attilio		Advance Forever/Eternal Youth	Conner Rosenkranz, NY
Piccirilli, Attilio		Leonardo Da Vinci	77 Sullivan Street
Piccirilli, Attilio		6 Mural Medallions	Morgan Library
Piccirilli, Ferruccio		Classical and floral designs	Custom House
Piccirilli, Ferruccio		Classical and floral designs	Courthse, 60 Centre St
Piccirilli, Attilio		A Soul	Spanierman G
Piccirilli, Attilio		Young Faun	Spanierman G
PBMCS	PBMCS	Capitols, north aisle O.T.	St. Bartholomew Ch.
PBMCS	PBMC	Capitols, south aisle N.T.	St. Bartholomew Ch.
Piccirilli, Attilio		Germany changed to Belgium	Custom House
Saint-Gaudens, A.	PBMCS	Children of Prescott H. Butler	MMA
Saint-Gaudens, A.	PBMCS	Children of Jacob H. Schiff	MMA
Saint-Gaudens, A.	PBMCS	Louise A. Gould, relief, 1893	MMA
Saint-Gaudens, A.	PBMCS	Louise A. Gould, bust, 1894	MMA
Saint-Gaudens, A.	PBMCS	Homer Saint-Gaudens	MMA
Saint-Gaudens, A.	PBMCS	Louise A. Gould, bust, 1904	MMA
Saint-Gaudens, A.	PBMCS	Frederick Thompson	Teachers College CU
Piccirilli, Masaniello		Classical and floral designs	Courthse, 60 Centre St

Piccirilli, Masaniello		Classical and floral designs	Custom House
Piccirilli, Guiseppe		Figures and decoration	Custom House
PBMCS	PBMCS	Capitols 8' 6"	Courthse, 60 CentreSt
Piccirilli, Bruno		Interior and exterior figures	Riverside Ch
Piccirilli, Orazio		Various	Riverside Ch
Piccirilli, Attilio		Front door	Riverside Ch
Piccirilli, Orazio		Interior decorations	Frick Museum
French, D.C.	PBMCS	Euripides	Low Library, CU
French, D.C.	PBMCS	Demosthenes	Low Library, CU
French, D.C.	PBMCS	Caesar	Low Library, CU
French, D.C.	PBMCS	Sophocles	Low Library, CU
Piccirilli, Attilio	PBMCS	St. Bartholomew, medal-2	Am.Numismatic Society
PBMCS	PBMCS	Andreas Vesalius	Riverside Ch. chancel
PBMCS	PBMCS	Joseph Lister	Riverside Ch. chancel
PBMCS	PBMCS	Robert Koch	Riverside Ch. chancel
PBMCS	PBMCS	Hippocrates	Riverside Ch. chancel
PBMCS	PBMCS	Luke	Riverside Ch. chancel
PBMCS	PBMCS	Christ the Physician	Riverside Ch. chancel
PBMCS	PBMCS	Thomas Sydenham	Riverside Ch. chancel
PBMCS	PBMCS	Louis Pasteur	Riverside Ch. chancel
PBMCS	PBMCS	Thomas Aquinas	Riverside Ch. chancel
PBMCS	PBMCS	Henry Drummond	Riverside Ch. chancel
PBMCS	PBMCS	Thomas Arnold	Riverside Ch. chancel
PBMCS	PBMCS	Socrates	Riverside Ch. chancel

PBMCS	PBMCS	Christ the Teacher	Riverside Ch. chancel
PBMCS	PBMCS	Desiderius Erasmus	Riverside Ch. chancel
PBMCS	PBMCS	Johann Heinrich Pestalozzi	Riverside Ch. chancel
PBMCS	PBMCS	Girolamo Savonarola	Riverside Ch. chancel
PBMCS	PBMCS	John Ruskin	Riverside Ch. chancel
PBMCS	PBMCS	Moses	Riverside Ch. chancel
PBMCS	PBMCS	Christ the Prophet	Riverside Ch. chancel
PBMCS	PBMCS	Isaiah	Riverside Ch. chancel
PBMCS	PBMCS	John the Baptist	Riverside Ch. chancel
PBMCS	PBMCS	Micah	Riverside Ch. chancel
PBMCS	PBMCS	Elijah	Riverside Ch. chancel
PBMCS	PBMCS	Elisha	Riverside Ch. chancel
PBMCS	PBMCS	Symbol	Riverside Ch. chancel
PBMCS	PBMCS	Symbol	Riverside Ch. chancel
PBMCS	PBMCS	Amos	Riverside Ch. chancel
PBMCS	PBMCS	Christ the Humanitarian	Riverside Ch. chancel
PBMCS	PBMCS	Francis of Assisi	Riverside Ch. chancel
PBMCS	PBMCS	Elizabeth of Hungary	Riverside Ch. chancel
PBMCS	PBMCS	Valentin Hauy	Riverside Ch. chancel
PBMCS	PBMCS	Ann Judson	Riverside Ch. chancel
PBMCS	PBMCS	Abraham Lincoln	Riverside Ch. chancel
PBMCS	PBMCS	Booker T. Washington	Riverside Ch. chancel
PBMCS	PBMCS	Samuel Chapman Armstrong	Riverside Ch. chancel
PBMCS	PBMCS	The Good Samaritan	Riverside Ch. chancel

PBMCS	PBMCS	Earl of Shaftesbury	Riverside Ch. chancel
PBMCS	PBMCS	Florence Nightingale	Riverside Ch. chancel
PBMCS	PBMCS	The Family Doctor	Riverside Ch. chancel
PBMCS	PBMCS	Walter Reed	Riverside Ch. chancel
PBMCS	PBMCS	Edward Jenner	Riverside Ch. chancel
PBMCS	PBMCS	Angel	Riverside Ch. chancel
PBMCS	PBMCS	Angel	Riverside Ch. chancel
PBMCS	PBMCS	John	Riverside Ch. chancel
PBMCS	PBMCS	William Booth	Riverside Ch. chancel
PBMCS	PBMCS	Mary the Mother of Jesus	Riverside Ch. chancel
PBMCS	PBMCS	John the Disciple	Riverside Ch. chancel
PBMCS	PBMCS	Philip the Evangelist	Riverside Ch. chancel
PBMCS	PBMCS	Stephen	Riverside Ch. chancel
PBMCS	PBMCS	John Eliot	Riverside Ch. chancel
PBMCS	PBMCS	Christ the Missionary	Riverside Ch. chancel
PBMCS	PBMCS	William Cary	Riverside Ch. chancel
PBMCS	PBMCS	Augustine	Riverside Ch. chancel
PBMCS	PBMCS	Francis Xavier	Riverside Ch. chancel
PBMCS	PBMCS	Robert Morrison	Riverside Ch. chancel
PBMCS	PBMCS	Adoniram Judson	Riverside Ch. chancel
PBMCS	PBMCS	Paul	Riverside Ch. chancel
PBMCS	PBMCS	David Livingston	Riverside Ch. chancel
PBMCS	PBMCS	Symbol	Riverside Ch. chancel
PBMCS	PBMCS	Symbol	Riverside Ch. chancel

PBMCS	PBMCS	George Fox	Riverside Ch. chancel
PBMCS	PBMCS	John Knox	Riverside Ch. chancel
PBMCS	PBMCS	John Wesley	Riverside Ch. chancel
PBMCS	PBMCS	Christ the Reformer	Riverside Ch. chancel
PBMCS	PBMCS	Martin Luther	Riverside Ch. chancel
PBMCS	PBMCS	John Calvin	Riverside Ch. chancel
PBMCS	PBMCS	John Greenleaf Whittier	Riverside Ch. chancel
PBMCS	PBMCS	Fra Angelico	Riverside Ch. chancel
PBMCS	PBMCS	John Milton	Riverside Ch. chancel
PBMCS	PBMCS	Giovanni Palestrina	Riverside Ch. chancel
PBMCS	PBMCS	Leonardo da Vinci	Riverside Ch. chancel
PBMCS	PBMCS	Michelangelo	Riverside Ch. chancel
PBMCS	PBMCS	Johann Sebastian Bach	Riverside Ch. chancel
PBMCS	PBMCS	Christ in Majesty	Riverside Ch tymp
PBMCS	PBMCS	Evangelical symbols	Riverside Ch tymp
PBMCS	PBMCS	A. panel-city scene	Riverside Ch tymp
PBMCS	PBMCS	A. panel-good v. evil	Riverside Ch tymp
PBMCS	PBMCS	B. panel-12 Apostles	Riverside Ch tymp
PBMCS	PBMCS	Isaiah, left of door	Riverside Ch
PBMCS	PBMCS	Jeremiah, left of door	Riverside Ch
PBMCS	PBMCS	Hosea, left of door	Riverside Ch
PBMCS	PBMCS	Amos, left of door	Riverside Ch
PBMCS	PBMCS	Micah, left of door	Riverside Ch
PBMCS	PBMCS	St. Simeon, right of door	Riverside Ch

PBMCS	PBMCS	St. Stephen, right of door	Riverside Ch
PBMCS	PBMCS	St. Paul, right of door	Riverside Ch
PBMCS	PBMCS	St. Barnabas, right of door	Riverside Ch
PBMCS	PBMCS	St. Timothy, right of door	Riverside Ch
PBMCS	PBMCS	St. John, bet. wood door	Riverside Ch
PBMCS	PBMCS	Outer ring- 16 angels	Riverside Ch
PBMCS	PBMCS	2nd ring-Hippocrates	Riverside Ch
PBMCS	PBMCS	2nd ring-Euclid	Riverside Ch
PBMCS	PBMCS	2nd ring- Archimedes	Riverside Ch
PBMCS	PBMCS	2nd ring-Hipparchus	Riverside Ch
PBMCS	PBMCS	2nd ring- Pare	Riverside Ch
PBMCS	PBMCS	2nd ring-Galileo	Riverside Ch
PBMCS	PBMCS	2nd ring- Kepler	Riverside Ch
PBMCS	PBMCS	2nd ring- Newton	Riverside Ch
PBMCS	PBMCS	2nd ring-Dalton	Riverside Ch
PBMCS	PBMCS	2nd ring-Faraday	Riverside Ch
PBMCS	PBMCS	2nd ring- Darwin	Riverside Ch
PBMCS	PBMCS	2nd ring- Pasteur	Riverside Ch
PBMCS	PBMCS	2nd ring- Lister	Riverside Ch
PBMCS	PBMCS	2nd ring- Albert Einstein	Riverside Ch
PBMCS	PBMCS	3rd ring-Pythagoras	Riverside Ch
PBMCS	PBMCS	3rd ring- Socrates	Riverside Ch
PBMCS	PBMCS	3rd ring- Plato	Riverside Ch
PBMCS	PBMCS	3rd ring- Epicurus	Riverside Ch

PBMCS	PBMCS	3rd ring- Aristotle	Riverside Ch
PBMCS	PBMCS	3rd ring- Seneca	Riverside Ch
PBMCS	PBMCS	3rd ring- Epictetus	Riverside Ch
PBMCS	PBMCS	3rd ring- Plotinus	Riverside Ch
PBMCS	PBMCS	3rd ring- Thomas Aquinas	Riverside Ch
PBMCS	PBMCS	3rd ring- Descartes	Riverside Ch
PBMCS	PBMCS	3rd ring- Benedict Spinoza	Riverside Ch
PBMCS	PBMCS	3rd ring- Immanuel Kant	Riverside Ch
PBMCS	PBMCS	3rd ring- Georg F. Hegel	Riverside Ch
PBMCS	PBMCS	3rd ring- Ralph W. Emerson	Riverside Ch
PBMCS	PBMCS	4th ring- Moses	Riverside Ch
PBMCS	PBMCS	4th ring- Confucius	Riverside Ch
PBMCS	PBMCS	4th ring- Buddha	Riverside Ch
PBMCS	PBMCS	4th ring- Mohammed	Riverside Ch
PBMCS	PBMCS	4th ring- Origen	Riverside Ch
PBMCS	PBMCS	4th ring- St. Francis of Assisi	Riverside Ch
PBMCS	PBMCS	4th ring- Aligheri Dante	Riverside Ch
PBMCS	PBMCS	4th ring- Balthazer Hubmeyer	Riverside Ch
PBMCS	PBMCS	4th ring- Martin Luther	Riverside Ch
PBMCS	PBMCS	4th ring- Calvin	Riverside Ch
PBMCS	PBMCS	4th ring- John Bunyan	Riverside Ch
PBMCS	PBMCS	4th ring- John Milton	Riverside Ch
PBMCS	PBMCS	4th ring- William Carey	Riverside Ch
PBMCS	PBMCS	4th ring- David Livingston	Riverside Ch

PBMCS	PBMCS	Inner arch- series of angels	Riverside Ch
Piccirilli, Attilio		St. Bartholomew, medal-2	Amer. Numismatic Soc.
PBMCS	PBMCS	Anna	Riverside Ch., pulpit
PBMCS	PBMCS	Amos	Riverside Ch., pulpit
PBMCS	PBMCS	Isaiah	Riverside Ch., pulpit
PBMCS	PBMCS	Hosea	Riverside Ch., pulpit
PBMCS	PBMCS	Miriam	Riverside Ch., pulpit
PBMCS	PBMCS	Nahum	Riverside Ch., pulpit
PBMCS	PBMCS	Toulouse, canopy	Riverside Ch., pulpit
PBMCS	PBMCS	Daniel	Riverside Ch., pulpit
PBMCS	PBMCS	Habakkuk	Riverside Ch., pulpit
PBMCS	PBMCS	Albi, canopy	Riverside Ch., pulpit
PBMCS	PBMCS	Obadiah	Riverside Ch., pulpit
PBMCS	PBMCS	Chartres, canopy	Riverside Ch., pulpit
PBMCS	PBMCS	Jeremiah	Riverside Ch., pulpit
PBMCS	PBMCS	Joel	Riverside Ch., pulpit
PBMCS	PBMCS	Coutances, canopy	Riverside Ch., pulpit
PBMCS	PBMCS	Jonah	Riverside Ch., pulpit
PBMCS	PBMCS	Paris, canopy	Riverside Ch., pulpit
PBMCS	PBMCS	Ezekiel	Riverside Ch., pulpit
PBMCS	PBMCS	Micah	Riverside Ch., pulpit
PBMCS	PBMCS	Rheims, canopy	Riverside Ch., pulpit
PBMCS	PBMCS	Zephaniah	Riverside Ch., pulpit
PBMCS	PBMCS	Hannah	Riverside Ch., pulpit

PBMCS	PBMCS	Bourges, canopy	Riverside Ch., pulpit
PBMCS	PBMCS	Haggai	Riverside Ch., pulpit
PBMCS	PBMCS	Amiens, canopy	Riverside Ch., pulpit
PBMCS	PBMCS	Zechariah	Riverside Ch., pulpit
PBMCS	PBMCS	Deborah	Riverside Ch., pulpit
PBMCS	PBMCS	Rouen, canopy	Riverside Ch., pulpit
PBMCS	PBMCS	Angel of Prophecy	Riverside Ch., pulpit
PBMCS	PBMCS	Widow's Mite, parable	Riverside Ch., pulpit
PBMCS	PBMCS	Tares and Wheat, parable	Riverside Ch., pulpit
PBMCS	PBMCS	Prayer, The Publican and Pharisee	Riverside, chancel rail
PBMCS	PBMCS	Prophecy, Isaiah the Lion, Lambs	Riverside, chancel rail
PBMCS	PBMCS	Evangelism, Paul on Mars Hill	Riverside, chancel rail
PBMCS	PBMCS	Ministery, Moses and Command.	Riverside, chancel rail
PBMCS	PBMCS	Ordination, Candidate and two elders	Riverside, chancel rail
PBMCS	PBMCS	Dedication, Parents, child, minister	Riverside, chancel rail
PBMCS	PBMCS	Memorial, Woman at tomb w. urn	Riverside, chancel rail
PBMCS	PBMCS	Baptism, Charlemagne, Bishop, Knight	Riverside, chancel rail
PBMCS	PBMCS	Communion,Christ,apostles, bread, wine	Riverside, chancel rail
PBMCS	PBMCS	Immortality, Christ, Mary in Garden	Riverside, chancel rail
PBMCS	PBMCS	Guardian Angel	Riverside, chancel rail
PBMCS	PBMCS	Old Law, Bondage of the law	Riverside, chancel rail
PBMCS	PBMCS	Guardian Angel	Riverside, chancel rail
PBMCS	PBMCS	Guardian Angel	Riverside, chancel rail
PBMCS	PBMCS	New Law, Liberty	Riverside, chancel rail

PBMCS	PBMCS	Creation, God and Adam	Riverside, chancel rail
PBMCS	PBMCS	Hymnody, Angel Trio	Riverside, chancel rail
PBMCS	PBMCS	Marriage, Priest and couple	Riverside, chancel rail
PBMCS	PBMCS	Festival, Triumphal entry	Riverside, chancel rail
PBMCS	PBMCS	Fellowship, David and Jonathan	Riverside, chancel rail
PBMCS	PBMCS	Patriotism, Joseph giving grain	Riverside, chancel rail
PBMCS	PBMCS	Sacrifice, Mary anointing Jesus	Riverside, chancel rail
PBMCS	PBMCS	Forgiveness,Christ and adultrous woman	Riverside chancel rail
PBMCS	PBMCS	New Testament, Sermon on Mount	Riverside, chancel rail
PBMCS	PBMCS	Old Testament, Ark of Covenant	Riverside, chancel rail
PBMCS	PBMCS	Lost Sheep, parable, stone lectern	Riverside Ch
PBMCS	PBMCS	Strasbourg, canopy, stone lectern	Riverside Ch
PBMCS	PBMCS	Wise Virgin, parable, stone lectern	Riverside Ch
PBMCS	PBMCS	Laon, canopy stone lectern	Riverside Ch
PBMCS	PBMCS	Mustard Seed, parable, stone lectern	Riverside Ch
PBMCS	PBMCS	Lepine, canopy stone lectern	Riverside Ch
PBMCS	PBMCS	Laborer in Vineyard, stone arm rest	Riverside Ch
PBMCS	PBMCS	Women w. Leaven, stone arm rest	Riverside Ch
PBMCS	PBMCS	From the Heavens, Ps.148,choir stall ends	Riverside Ch
PBMCS	PBMCS	All His Angels, Ps.148, choir stall ends	Riverside Ch
PBMCS	PBMCS	All His Hosts, Ps.148, choir stall ends	Riverside Ch
PBMCS	PBMCS	Sun, Ps.148, choir stall ends	Riverside Ch
PBMCS	PBMCS	Moon+Stars, Ps.148, choir stall ends	Riverside Ch
PBMCS	PBMCS	Waters Above Heavens, choir stall ends	Riverside Ch

PBMCS	PBMCS	From the Earth, Ps.148, choir stall ends	Riverside Ch
PBMCS	PBMCS	Dragon, Ps.148, choir stall ends	Riverside Ch
PBMCS	PBMCS	Deeps, Ps.148, choir stall ends	Riverside Ch
PBMCS	PBMCS	Fire, Ps. 148, choir stall ends	Riverside Ch
PBMCS	PBMCS	Hail+Snow, Ps.148, choir stall ends	Riverside Ch
PBMCS	PBMCS	Wind, Ps.148, choir stall ends	Riverside Ch
PBMCS	PBMCS	Hills+Mountains, Ps.148,choir stall ends	Riverside Ch
PBMCS	PBMCS	Fruitful Trees, Ps.148, choir stall ends	Riverside Ch
PBMCS	PBMCS	Cedars, Ps.148, choir stall ends	Riverside Ch
PBMCS	PBMCS	Beasts+Cattle, Ps.148, choir stall ends	Riverside Ch
PBMCS	PBMCS	Creeping Things, Ps.148,choir stall ends	Riverside Ch
PBMCS	PBMCS	Flying Things, Ps.148, choir stall ends	Riverside Ch
PBMCS	PBMCS	Kings, Ps.148, choir stall ends	Riverside Ch
PBMCS	PBMCS	Princes, Ps.148, choir stall ends	Riverside Ch
PBMCS	PBMCS	Judges, P.148, choir stall ends	Riverside Ch
PBMCS	PBMCS	Praise Ye the Lord, Ps.148,choir stall ends	Riverside Ch
PBMCS	PBMCS	Youths+Maidens, Ps.148,choir stall ends	Riverside Ch
PBMCS	PBMCS	Children+Old Men, Ps.148,choir stall ends	Riverside Ch
PBMCS	PBMCS	Fall, Ps.148, front choir rail ends	Riverside Ch
PBMCS	PBMCS	Winter, Ps.148, front choir rail ends	Riverside Ch
PBMCS	PBMCS	Spring, Ps.148, front choir rail ends	Riverside Ch
PBMCS	PBMCS	Summer, Ps.148, front choir rail ends	Riverside Ch
PBMCS	PBMCS	Singing Angels, Ps.148, choir end arm rest	Riverside Ch
PBMCS	PBMCS	Scientist, Ps.148, choir end arm rests	Riverside Ch

PBMCS	PBMCS	Archaeologist+Geologist,Ps.148	Riverside Ch
PBMCS	PBMCS	Explorer+Inventor, Ps.148, choir end arm	Riverside Ch
PBMCS	PBMCS	Laborer, Ps.148, choir end arm rests	Riverside Ch
PBMCS	PBMCS	Naturalist, Ps.148, choir end arm rests	Riverside Ch
PBMCS	PBMCS	Historian, Ps.148, choir end arm rests	Riverside Ch
PBMCS	PBMCS	Singing Angel, Ps.148, choir end arm rests	Riverside Ch
PBMCS	PBMCS	Building Sky, Ps.104, choir Miseri	Riverside Ch
PBMCS	PBMCS	Hand of God, Ps.104 , choir Miseri	Riverside Ch
PBMCS	PBMCS	Building of Earth, Ps.104, choir Miseri	Riverside Ch
PBMCS	PBMCS	Time, Ps.104, choir Miseri	Riverside Ch
PBMCS	PBMCS	Chariot of Clouds, Ps.104, choir Miseri	Riverside Ch
PBMCS	PBMCS	Angel with Winged Feet, Ps.104 choir Miseri	Riverside Ch
PBMCS	PBMCS	Foundation of Earth, Ps.104choirMiseri	Riverside Ch
PBMCS	PBMCS	Angel with Vial, Ps.104 choir Miseri	Riverside Ch
PBMCS	PBMCS	Flood, Ps.104, choir Miseri	Riverside Ch
PBMCS	PBMCS	Dove with Olive Branch,Ps.104 choir	Riverside Ch
PBMCS	PBMCS	Ebb with Rainbow, Ps.104,choir Miseri	Riverside Ch
PBMCS	PBMCS	Beast Drinking, Ps.104, choir Miseri	Riverside Ch
PBMCS	PBMCS	River with Trees, Ps.104, choir Miseri	Riverside Ch
PBMCS	PBMCS	Birds in Trees, Ps.104, choir Miseri	Riverside Ch
PBMCS	PBMCS	Fruitful trees, Ps.104, choir Miseri	Riverside Ch
PBMCS	PBMCS	Mother and child, Ps.104, choir Miseri	Riverside Ch
PBMCS	PBMCS	Archangel Michael, Ps.104,choir Miseri	Riverside Ch
PBMCS	PBMCS	Messenger, Ps.104, choir Miseri	Riverside Ch

PBMCS	PBMCS	Warrior, Ps.104, choir Miseri	Riverside Ch
PBMCS	PBMCS	Artisan, Ps.104, choir Miseri	Riverside Ch
PBMCS	PBMCS	Shepherd, Ps.104, choir Miseri	Riverside Ch
PBMCS	PBMCS	Woodman, Ps. 104, choir Miseri	Riverside Ch
PBMCS	PBMCS	Archangel Uriel, Ps.104, choir Miseri	Riverside Ch
PBMCS	PBMCS	Workman, Ps.104, choir Miseri	Riverside Ch
PBMCS	PBMCS	Builder, Ps.104, choir Miseri	Riverside Ch
PBMCS	PBMCS	Mariner, Ps.104, choir Miseri	Riverside Ch
PBMCS	PBMCS	Archangel Gabriel, Ps.104, choir Miseri	Riverside Ch
PBMCS	PBMCS	Man, Ps.104, choir Miseri	Riverside Ch
PBMCS	PBMCS	Vineyard & Wine, Ps.104, choir Miseri	Riverside Ch
PBMCS	PBMCS	Olive Tree Oil, Ps.104, choir Miseri	Riverside Ch
PBMCS	PBMCS	Maize & Bread, Ps.104, choir Miseri	Riverside Ch
PBMCS	PBMCS	Stork Nest in Tree, Ps.104,choir Miseri	Riverside Ch
PBMCS	PBMCS	Hills, Rabbits & Goats, Ps.104, choir	Riverside Ch
PBMCS	PBMCS	Night, Ps.104, choir Miseri	Riverside Ch
PBMCS	PBMCS	Sleep, Ps.104, choir Miseri	Riverside Ch
PBMCS	PBMCS	Day, Ps.104, choir Miseri	Riverside Ch
PBMCS	PBMCS	Work, Ps.104,choir Miseri	Riverside Ch
PBMCS	PBMCS	Ship, Ps.104, choir Miseri	Riverside Ch
PBMCS	PBMCS	Sea, Ps.104, choir Miseri	Riverside Ch
PBMCS	PBMCS	Life, Ps.104, choir Miseri	Riverside Ch
PBMCS	PBMCS	Birth, Ps.104, choir Miseri	Riverside Ch
PBMCS	PBMCS	Death, Ps.104, choir Miseri	Riverside Ch

PBMCS	PBMCS	Re-Birth, Ps.104, choir Miseri	Riverside Ch
PBMCS	PBMCS	Naomi, Ps.104 ,prie dieu	Riverside Ch
PBMCS	PBMCS	Boaz, Ps.104, prie dieu	Riverside Ch
PBMCS	PBMCS	Ruth, Ps.104, prie dieu	Riverside Ch
PBMCS	PBMCS	Nave pillars-Jeremiah Capitals	Riverside Ch
PBMCS	PBMCS	Moses, Front of first gallery	Riverside Ch
PBMCS	PBMCS	Amos, Front of first gallery	Riverside Ch
PBMCS	PBMCS	David, Front of first gallery	Riverside Ch
PBMCS	PBMCS	Gideon, Front of first gallery	Riverside Ch
PBMCS	PBMCS	John Chrysostom,Nave niches	Riverside Ch
PBMCS	PBMCS	St. Augustine, Nave niches	Riverside Ch
PBMCS	PBMCS	Girolamo Savonarola, Nave niches	Riverside Ch
PBMCS	PBMCS	Hugh Latimer, nave niches	Riverside Ch
PBMCS	PBMCS	John Wesley, Nave niches	Riverside Ch
PBMCS	PBMCS	Phillips Brooks, Nave niches	Riverside Ch
PBMCS	PBMCS	Exterior of chapel door	Riverside Ch
PBMCS	BMCS	Child at birth-Chapel door exterior	Riverside Ch
PBMCS	PBMCS	Growing child-Chapel door exterior	Riverside Ch
PBMCS	PBMCS	Maturity-Chapel door exterior	Riverside Ch
PBMCS	PBMCS	Marriage-Chapel door exterior	Riverside Ch
PBMCS	PBMCS	Birth of new child-Chapel door ext	Riverside Ch
PBMCS	PBMCS	Good-bracket-Chapel door exterior	Riverside Ch
PBMCS	PBMCS	Evil-bracket-Chapel door exterior	Riverside Ch
PBMCS	PBMCS	Air-column symbols-Chapel door	Riverside Ch

PBMCS	PBMCS	Ether-column symbols-Chapel door	Riverside Ch
PBMCS	PBMCS	Fire-column symbols-Chapel door	Riverside Ch
PBMCS	PBMCS	Water-column symbols-Chapel door	Riverside Ch
PBMCS	PBMCS	Scribes-4, Chapel door ext columns	Riverside Ch
PBMCS	PBMCS	Zodiac-12, Chapel door, arch rings	Riverside Ch
PBMCS	PBMCS	David-above main door	Riverside Ch
PBMCS	PBMCS	Solomon-above main door	Riverside Ch
PBMCS	PBMCS	Marcus Aurelius-above main door	Riverside Ch
PBMCS	PBMCS	Clovis-above main door	Riverside Ch
PBMCS	PBMCS	Constantine-above main door	Riverside Ch
PBMCS	PBMCS	Charlemagne-above main door	Riverside Ch
PBMCS	PBMCS	Alfred-above main door	Riverside Ch
PBMCS	PBMCS	St. Gabriel-corner of tower niche	Riverside Ch
PBMCS	PBMCS	St. Raphael-corner of tower niche	Riverside Ch
PBMCS	PBMCS	St. Uriel-corner of tower niche	Riverside Ch
PBMCS	PBMCS	St. Michael-corner of tower niche	Riverside Ch
PBMCS	PBMCS	Angel w. cathedral-125th St.apse	Riverside Ch
PBMCS	PBMCS	Angel w. book-125th St. apse	Riverside Ch
PBMCS	PBMCS	Angel w. seal-125th St. apse	Riverside Ch
PBMCS	PBMCS	Angel w. censer-125th St.apse	Riverside Ch
PBMCS	PBMCS	Angel w. trumpet-125th St.apse	Riverside Ch
PBMCS	PBMCS	Angel w. rainbow-125th St.apse	Riverside Ch
PBMCS	PBMCS	Resurrection Angel-ridge pole, roof	Riverside Ch
PBMCS	PBMCS	Mary-Woman's Porch	Riverside Ch

PBMCS	PBMCS	Martha-Woman's Porch	Riverside Ch
PBMCS	PBMCS	Eunice-Woman's Porch	Riverside Ch
PBMCS	PBMCS	Lois-Woman's Porch	Riverside Ch
PBMCS	PBMCS	Dove-door, Woman's Porch	Riverside Ch
PBMCS	PBMCS	Pelican-door, Woman's Porch	Riverside Ch
PBMCS	PBMCS	Passion Flower-door, Woman's Porch	Riverside Ch
PBMCS	PBMCS	Swan-door, Woman's Porch	Riverside Ch
PBMCS	PBMCS	Columbine-door, Woman's Porch	Riverside Ch
PBMCS	PBMCS	Beehive-door, Woman's Porch	Riverside Ch
PBMCS	PBMCS	Strawberry-door, Woman's Porch	Riverside Ch
PBMCS	PBMCS	Lily-door, Woman's Porch	Riverside Ch
PBMCS	PBMCS	Peacock-door, Woman's Porch	Riverside Ch
PBMCS	PBMCS	Violet-door, Woman's Porch	Riverside Ch
PBMCS	PBMCS	Butterfly-door, Woman's Porch	Riverside Ch
PBMCS	PBMCS	Ant-door Woman's Porch	Riverside Ch
PBMCS	PBMCS	Daisy-door, Woman's Porch	Riverside Ch
PBMCS	PBMCS	Owl-door, Woman's Porch	Riverside Ch
PBMCS	PBMCS	Rose-door, Woman's Porch	Riverside Ch
PBMCS	PBMCS	Heron-door, Woman's Porch	Riverside Ch
PBMCS	PBMCS	Hen with Chicks-door, Woman's P.	Riverside Ch
PBMCS	PBMCS	St. Paul-Cloister Entrance	Riverside Ch
PBMCS	PBMCS	St. Francis-Cloister Entrance	Riverside Ch
PBMCS	PBMCS	St. Martin-Cloister Entrance	Riverside Ch
PBMCS	PBMCS	Masseiah-beside Cloister Entrance	Riverside Ch

PBMCS	PBMCS	Lord's Supper, chapel reredo	Riverside Ch
PBMCS	PBMCS	Transfiguration, chapel reredo	Riverside Ch
PBMCS	PBMCS	Figures-2,chapel, right niche above	Riverside Ch
PBMCS	PBMCS	Angel, chapel, right niche above	Riverside Ch
PBMCS	PBMCS	Figures-2, chapel, left niche above	Riverside Ch
PBMCS	PBMCS	Angel, chapel, left niche above	Riverside Ch
PBMCS	PBMCS	Altar front, chapel-20	Riverside Ch
PBMCS	PBMCS	Altar front, chapel, animals-5	Riverside Ch
PBMCS	PBMCS	Bull, piano recess, chapel	Riverside Ch
PBMCS	PBMCS	Devil, piano recess, chapel	Riverside Ch
PBMCS	PBMCS	Doorway, chapel-2	Riverside Ch
PBMCS	PBMCS	Nave, rear door, chapel-5	Riverside Ch
PBMCS	PBMCS	Nave, organ loft, chapel-ca 15	Riverside Ch
PBMCS	PBMCS	Nave, decorated capitals, chapel-30	Riverside Ch
PBMCS	PBMCS	Nave, main church, capitals, left-35	Riverside Ch
PBMCS	PBMCS	Nave,main church, capitals rt -35	Riverside Ch
PBMCS	PBMCS	Martin Luther-above portal W. front	St. Bart's Ch.
PBMCS	PBMCS	St. Paul-above portal west front	St. Bart's Ch.
PBMCS	PBMCS	St. Francis of Assisi-portal west frnt	St. Bart's Ch.
PBMCS	PBMCS	Phillips Brooks-above portal west frnt	St. Bart's Ch.
PBMCS	PBMCS	Ark (Noah) -tracery, west front	St. Bart's Ch.
PBMCS	PBMCS	Lion (Joel) -tracery, west front	St. Bart's Ch.
PBMCS	PBMCS	Fiery Chariot (Elijah), tracery w. front	St. Bart's Ch.
PBMCS	PBMCS	Turreted Gate (Ezekiel) tracery, w. fr	St. Bart's Ch.

PBMCS	PBMCS	Angel (Malachi)-tracery west front	St. Bart's Ch.
PBMCS	PBMCS	Sword (Isaiah)-tracery west front	St. Bart's Ch.
PBMCS	PBMCS	Temple (Zechariah)-tracery west front	St. Bart's Ch.
PBMCS	PBMCS	Gourd (Jonah)-tracery west front	St. Barts Ch.
PBMCS	PBMCS	Wand in hand (Jeremiah)-tracery w.	St. Bart's Ch.
PBMCS	PBMCS	Ram with horns (Daniel)-tracery w.	St. Bart's Ch.
PBMCS	PBMCS	Shepherd's crook (Amos)-tracery w.	St. Bart's Ch.
PBMCS	PBMCS	Christ healing the sick-north porch	St. Bart's Ch.
PBMCS	PBMCS	St. Luke-north porch	St. Bart's Ch.
PBMCS	PBMCS	Dorcas-north porch	St. Bart's Ch.
PBMCS	PBMCS	St. Bartholomew-wheel window	St. Bart's Ch.
PBMCS	PBMCS	St. Philip-wheel window	St. Bart's Ch.
PBMCS	PBMCS	St. Athanasius-narthex, capitals	St. Bart's Ch.
PBMCS	PBMCS	Pope Gregory I-narthex, capitals	St. Bart's Ch.
PBMCS	PBMCS	Thomas Cranmer-narthex, capitals	St. Bart's Ch.
PBMCS	PBMCS	Bishop William White-narthex, cap.	St. Bart's Ch.
PBMCS	PBMCS	Florence Nightingale-narthex, cap.	St. Bart's Ch.
PBMCS	PBMCS	George Wiliams-narthex, capital	St. Bart's Ch.
PBMCS	PBMCS	St. Clement of Alexander-narthex	St. Bart's Ch.
PBMCS	PBMCS	St. John Chrysostom-narthex, cap.	St. Bart's Ch.
PBMCS	PBMCS	John Wyclif of Lutterworth-narthex	St. Bart's Ch.
PBMCS	PBMCS	John Wesley-narthex, capital	St. Bart's Ch.
PBMCS	PBMCS	Wm. Augustus Muhlenberg-narth.	St. Bart's Ch.
PBMCS	PBMCS	The Creation, left aisle, capital	St. Bart's Ch.

PBMCS	PBMCS	Temptation and Fall of Man, lt. aisle	St. Bart's Ch.
PBMCS	PBMCS	The Flood, left aisle capital	St. Bart's Ch.
PBMCS	PBMCS	Abraham Sacrificing Isaac left .aisle	St. Bart's Ch.
PBMCS	PBMCS	Joseph and his brethern, lt.aisle cap	St. Bart's Ch.
PBMCS	PBMCS	Moses and burning bush,left aisle	St. Bart's Ch.
PBMCS	PBMCS	Crossing the Red Sea, left aisle	St. Bart's Ch.
PBMCS	PBMCS	The Law of Moses, left aisle capital	St. Bart's Ch.
PBMCS	PBMCS	Christ on the Mount, rt. aisle cap.	St. Bart's Ch.
PBMCS	PBMCS	The Resurrection, right aisle capital	St. Bart's Ch.
PBMCS	PBMCS	The Transfiguration, right aisle cap.	St. Bart's Ch.
PBMCS	PBMCS	Christ and Disciples, rt. aisle capital	St. Bart's Ch.
PBMCS	PBMCS	Raising of Lazarus, rt. aisle capital	St. Bart's Ch.
PBMCS	PBMCS	Christ walking on water, rt. aisle cap	St. Bart's Ch.
PBMCS	PBMCS	Temptation of Christ, rt. aisle cap.	St. Bart's Ch.
PBMCS	PBMCS	The Nativity, right aisle capital	St. Bart's Ch.
PBMCS	PBMCS	Chapel capitals, left side-19 scenes	St. Bart's Ch.
PBMCS	PBMCS	Chapel capitals,right side-26 scenes	St. Bart's Ch.
Piccirilli, Attilio		Leonardo Da Vinci	Tiro A. Segno 27 Mac Dougal St.

3. Piccirilli sculpture in Brooklyn

The first column has the name of the sculptor. The second column has the carver's name. A blank space in the second column indicates that we assume the sculptor carved the piece. The third column has the name of the sculpture and the fourth its general location.

SCULPTOR	CARVER	TITLE	LOCATION
Piccirilli, Attilio	PBMCS	Indian Law Giver	Bklyn. Museum
Piccirilli, Attilio	PBMCS	Indian Literature	Bklyn. Museum
Gelert, Johannes S.	PBMCS	Roman Emperor	Bklyn. Museum
Bitter, Karl	PBMCS	Chinese Art	Bklyn. Museum
Bitter, Karl	PBMCS	Chinese Law	Bklyn. Museum
Bitter, Karl	PBMCS	Chinese Philosophy	Bklyn. Museum
Bitter, Karl	PBMCS	Chinese Religion	Bklyn. Museum
Gelert, Johannes S.	PBMCS	Roman Orator	Bklyn. Museum
Heber Carl A.	PBMCS	Epic Poetry	Bklyn. Museum
Keck, Charles	PBMCS	Genius of Islam	Bklyn. Museum
Adams, Herbert	PBMCS	Greek Architecture	Bklyn. Museum
Brewster, George T.	PBMCS	Greek Drama	Bklyn. Museum
French, D.C.	PBMCS	Greek Epic	Bklyn. Museum
Adams, Herbert	PBMCS	Greek Letters	Bklyn. Museum
French, D.C.	PBMCS	Greek Lyric Poetry	Bklyn. Museum

Adams, Herbert	PBMCS	Greek Philosophy	Bklyn. Museum
French, D.C.	PBMCS	Greek Religion	Bklyn. Museum
Cox, Kenyon	PBMCS	Greek Science	Bklyn. Museum
Adams, Herbert	PBMCS	Greek Sculpture	Bklyn. Museum
Brewster, George T.	PBMCS	Greek State	Bklyn. Museum
Lukeman, Augus	PBMCS	Hebrew Apostle	Bklyn. Museum
Lukeman, Augustus	PBMCS	Hebrew Law Giver	Bklyn. Museum
Lukeman, Augustus	PBMCS	Hebrew Prophet	Bklyn. Museum
Lukeman, Augustus	PBMCS	Hebrew Psalmist	Bklyn. Museum
Potter, Edward, C.	PBMCS	Indian Philosophy	Bklyn. Museum
Potter, Edward, C.	PBMCS	Indian Religion	Bklyn. Museum
Scudder, Janet	PBMCS	Japanese Art	Bklyn. Museum
Gelert, Johannes S.	PBMCS	Roman Statesman	Bklyn. Museum
Gelert, Johannes S.	PBMCS	Roman Law Giver	Bklyn. Museum
Quinn, Edmond T.	PBMCS	Persian Philosophy	Bklyn. Museum
French, D.C.	PBMCS	Science and Art, pediment	Bklyn. Museum
PBMCS	PBMCS	Williamsburg W.W.I Mem.	Brooklyn, N.Y.
French, D.C.	PBMCS	Manhattan	Bklyn. Museum
PBMCS	PBMCS	Bklyn Daily Eagle's eagle	Main Branch, Bklyn Public Library
Saint-Gaudens, A.	PBMCS	Homer Saint-Gaudens	Bklyn. Museum
French, D.C.	PBMCS	Brooklyn	Bklyn. Museum

4. Piccirilli sculpture in Queens

The first column has the name of the sculptor. The second column has the carver's name. A blank space in the second column indicates that we assume the sculptor carved the piece. The third column has the name of the sculpture and the fourth its general location.

SCULPTOR	CARVER	TITLE	LOCATION
MacMonnies, Fred.	PBMCS	Civic Virtue	Queens Blvd+UnionTp
Piccirilli, Attilio		Thomas Jefferson, bust	Queens College

www.ingramcontent.com/pod-product-compliance
Lightning Source LLC
LaVergne TN
LVHW020637100826
845148LV00012B/2219

9780970340320